Tunes Teach

By Kris Thurgood and Kim Christopherson

Cover Illustration by Jennifer Emery
Inside Illustrations by Janet Armbrust

Published by Instructional Fair • TS Denison
an imprint of
McGraw-Hill Children's Publishing

About the Authors

Kris Thurgood and Kim Christopherson, twin sisters, are natives of southern California. After graduating from Ricks College, they transferred to Utah State University to pursue degrees in elementary education. They both graduated from the College of Education in June 1995. After teaching fourth-grade children for several years in different school districts, they spent two years as team teachers for the same fourth grade classroom. Currently, they are also active as workshop presenters, sharing their creative and fun ideas in education at many local, state, and university workshops to teachers from all over the country.

Dedication

To our husbands, Mike and Ryan, and to all our former students who made us realize that teaching through music is fun and effective

Credits

Authors: Kris Thurgood and Kim Christopherson
Cover Illustration: Jennifer Emery
Inside Illustrations: Janet Armbrust
Project Director: Debra Olson Pressnall
Cover Art Direction: Peter Lochner
Editors: Debra Olson Pressnall and Karen Seberg
Graphic Layout and Icon Art: Mark Conrad

Acknowledgments

We would like to thank the following teachers who implemented these songs in their classrooms and provided us with valuable feedback: Dana White, Brenda Bilodeau, Bonnie Bickers, Suzie Macriss, Deaun Lape, Mindee Larsen, Kandyce Earl, Callie Ball, Peggy Tuddenham, Roseann Porter, Jan Lindley, Susan Nielsen, and Luann Purser. We would also like to show appreciation to Bill Lindauer, Heather Mons, Jill Richins, and both of our families for their support and encouragement.

McGraw-Hill Children's Publishing
A Division of The ***McGraw-Hill*** *Companies*

Send all other inquiries to
McGraw-Hill Children's Publishing
3195 Wilson Drive NW
Grand Rapids, Michigan 49544

Printed in the United States of America

Tunes That Teach
ISBN: 0-7424-0120-0

1 2 3 4 5 6 7 8 9 05 04 03 02 01

Table of Contents

Introduction

Welcome!

This book has been designed for both parents and teachers. As teachers, we have come to acknowledge the role of music in connection with memorization of important facts. For many of us, it is much easier to recall information that is stored in our memories through songs. This is the reason why we wrote *Tunes That Teach*. In an effort to help our students learn information quickly, we wrote lyrics about basic concepts that are sung to familiar tunes. Not only did our students learn, but they had fun with the music! It is our hope that you will utilize *Tunes That Teach* in the best way possible for your unique situation. After all, you know your students best!

At the Introduction of a New Unit

Music is an excellent venue to get children immediately involved in a new unit of study. What would the students think if they saw their teacher marching in rhythm to the song "Days of the Week" using the tune of the "Army Cadence"? As students echo each line with their teacher, they automatically know what they will learn—the days of the week. Other examples of songs include "I'm Just a Little Raindrop" which introduces students to the water cycle, "Cool Geometry" which covers lines and angles, and "Mental and Physical Exercise" which emphasizes ways to stay healthy.

A Review of Concepts Before Taking a Test

Before taking a test, have the students review songs from that unit of study. Students can even review all songs before end-of-level testing. For example, a third grade class completed a unit on simple machines. A question on the test asked for an example of a simple screw. The teacher simply reminded her students to remember the song they had learned. One boy in the class sang the song in his head and immediately came up with a correct answer!

These songs can be a powerful tool for helping students recall important information. Help your students feel successful! Review any songs you can with them before taking a test.

Children Teach Their Families

We know that in many learning situations the teacher often learns and understands more than the students. So, why not turn your students into teachers? As a homework assignment, have your students teach their families a song they learned that day. Students will have fun teaching new songs, and parents will appreciate knowing what their children are learning in school. This type of homework assignment becomes a great way to involve parents in the learning process.

Use as a Model for Students to Write Their Own Songs

Depending upon the grade you teach and the skill level of your students, have them write their own songs. Students may find writing their own songs very rewarding.

When teaching younger students, for example, write the lyrics for the song on chart paper. Show a word in the song and ask, "What other word could we use in its place?" For example, in the song "We Need Water," change the words about animals needing water to a song about why the earth or humans need water.

For older students, divide a unit into more specific concepts. For example, if you were studying a unit on weather, each verse could address a specific topic like clouds, weather tools, or the water cycle. Have student groups brainstorm ideas about their topics. Nex, assign a "tune" so the students can unite their ideas with a melody! Perhaps your class is studying famous people in history, then encourage the students to write songs about different people using familiar tunes.

Imagine the sense of satisfaction your students will feel when they get in front of the class and teach other students their new song!

Sing Songs on Long Bus Rides

With *Tunes That Teach*, you can make the time on a field trip more enjoyable as well as instructional. Long trips on the bus will seem to take less time for everyone when singing songs together. To add more interest, have students choose the "style" of voices they would like to use. For example, first have the students sing in their best "opera" voices. Next, students can sing in their sweetest "baby" voices. And finally, they can sing in their deepest "football player" voices. The possibilities are endless, and students will never get bored choosing their different voices! Singing the songs in rounds is another delightful way to pass the time. The best part is, the students continue repeating the concepts without even realizing that learning is taking place!

Illustrate Mini-Books Using the Songs

Using *Tunes That Teach* songs to illustrate books can be an individual or class project. If done as a class, assign each student or group of students a line of the song. They are then responsible for writing and illustrating what that line means on a sheet of white construction paper. Collect all of the pages and bind them with plastic spiral binding, yarn, or even staples. You now have a new addition to your classroom library!

Add Actions to Songs

Having the students do actions while singing the songs encourages them to participate in more than one way. Marching or skipping to the beat are ways to involve movement. For the song "Cool Geometry," have the students make parallel and intersecting lines with their arms to reinforce the concepts. Of course, one of the best ways to involve the children is to have them create their own actions to songs. We promise they will come up with some fun and creative ways to act out their ideas! We have also included suggestions of actions for most songs that you can use.

In Conclusion, You May Be Asking, "How Do I Teach These Songs?"

Well, from personal experience, we can offer several techniques for you to use when teaching the words to these tunes.

The easiest and most inexpensive way is to simply sing one line at a time and have the students repeat it. Copying the song onto chart paper or displaying it on an overhead screen also makes learning the words easier. Since these tunes are already familiar to the majority of your students, you may not have to do the leading after all! Let the kids take over, and they may just lead you!

In our classroom, we also made song folders by folding 18 x 22 inch (46 x 51 cm) sheets of construction paper in half. These collection folders serve as efficient tools for storing the songs if you choose to distribute copies to each student. When you have an extra five minutes before lunch or at the end of the day, students can quickly take out their folders and pick favorite songs to sing. Perhaps at the end of the school year, you can bind their songs together in booklets and give them to the students as keepsakes!

Also provided for the songs are teacher suggestions. These are ideas you may use while singing the songs or enrichment activities to further your study of the concept learned in the song. Some songs even include follow-up activities for you to use. Hopefully, these ideas will benefit you in your classroom and help students to retain knowledge longer. We also hope that you will have fun and enjoy the excitement that comes through music in the classroom! Best of luck!

Teacher Tips and Suggestions

for Health Tunes

Calcium Builds Strong Bones and Teeth (Page 9)

Lead students in actions to "make muscles" and then point to their teeth during the line "bones and teeth" on the first and third verses. During the second verse, call five students to the front of the room and have them hold pictures of food that provide calcium. They can hold up their pictures when the foods are mentioned. Challenge your students to name even more foods that contain calcium. Can they fit their new words into the tune?

The Cardiovascular System (Page 10)

Photocopy pattern page 11 for the students to color. If interested, also copy the diagram on an overhead transparency and display it while singing the song. Talk about the parts of the cardiovascular system. If possible, locate a diagram that shows the four chambers of the heart: left ventricle, right ventricle, left atrium, and right atrium.

The Digestive System (Page 12)

Make an overhead transparency of the picture of the digestive system (see page 13), then display it. While singing, take a pointer stick and follow down through the digestive tract. Call different students to the front of the classroom and have them do the same thing with the pointer stick while the class sings the song several times.

Disease Prevention (Page 14)

Follow each action as instructed on the song page. Invite a professional from your local health department to discuss these steps of disease prevention.

Human Development and Relationships (Page 15)

Call two students to the front of the room to act out what comes to their minds when their classmates are singing the song.

Identifying and Developing Our Talents (Page 16)

Give each student a copy of "My Many Talents" (see page 17). Have the students complete the diagram by recording their different talents. Students may enjoy exchanging their papers with friends and asking them to fill in some of the blanks. Follow up with a class talent show!

Mental and Physical Exercise (Page 18)

Follow each action as instructed on the song page. Discuss with your students other ways to stay mentally and physically fit.

Teacher Tips and Suggestions, Cont.

My Five Senses (Page 19)

Point to the different body parts as they are mentioned in the song. As a follow-up activity, have students complete the "My Five Senses" booklet (see pages 20 and 21). Students can draw or cut out pictures from magazines to paste onto the different pages. Another idea is to glue on some actual objects to the pages. For example, the student can glue a gum wrapper on the "Things I Can Taste" page or glue pressed tree leaves on the "Things I Can Touch" page. When the pages are complete, cut them apart on the dashed lines and assembled them to make the booklet. Use either a stapler or hole punch and yarn to secure the pages together.

Resolving Conflict (Page 22)

Call two students to the front of the room to act out each different verse while the class is singing.

The Skeletal System (Page 24)

Tell students to point to the different parts of their bodies as they sing. *Tip:* When singing the chorus, speed up the tempo of the song. If interested, copy the pattern page (see page 25) onto an overhead transparency. Then display the diagram while introducing the bones in the body. If appropriate, identify some of the bones by using their correct scientific names. Also identify the different types of joints in the body, such as ball and socket (hip and shoulder) and hinge (elbow and knee).

Stress Management (Page 26)

As a follow-up activity, make a chart for each student to take home and hang in his/her bedroom. Examples of tasks included on the chart: make the bed, keep the bedroom tidy, finish homework, eat healthful snacks, and so on. The charts will remind students about those things they need to be doing each day to manage their stress.

Calcium Builds Strong Bones and Teeth

Tune "Mary Had a Little Lamb"

Calcium builds strong bones and teeth, (Point to muscles, then teeth.)
Bones and teeth, (Point to muscles, then teeth.)
Bones and teeth. (Point to muscles, then teeth.)
Calcium builds strong bones and teeth (Point to muscles, then teeth.)
For a healthy body! (Put hands on hips, nod head.)

We can find it in yogurt and cheese,
Yogurt and cheese,
Yogurt and cheese.
We can find it in yogurt and cheese,
Broccoli, milk, and ice cream!

Calcium builds strong bones and teeth, (Point to muscles, then teeth.)
Bones and teeth, (Point to muscles, then teeth.)
Bones and teeth. (Point to muscles, then teeth.)
Calcium builds strong bones and teeth (Point to muscles, then teeth.)
For a healthy body! (Put hands on hips, nod head.)

The Cardiovascular System

"Battle Hymn of the Republic" Tune

My heart is a muscle that expands and contracts.
(Squeeze hands back and forth.)

It pumps my blood and is found in the middle of my chest.
(Pound chest.)

It beats a little faster when I run, than when I rest.
(Run in place.)

Four chambers are in my heart!
(Hold up two fingers.)

Chorus: (March in place throughout chorus.)

My heart! My heart is a strong muscle
That works even faster when I hustle.
It grows as I grow.
It makes the blood flow.
I try to be heart smart!

The left ventricle's larger and sends blood to all my parts.
(Show muscles.)

The right one is smaller and pumps it only to my lungs.
(Take deep breath in.)

Above these two large chambers are two smaller ones.
These are called atria!

Repeat Chorus (March in place throughout chorus.)

Now my cardiovascular system consists of more than just my heart,
I have blood vessels called arteries that are a central part.
There are also veins and capillaries to send the blood "a-flow."
All of these things you should know!
(Point to audience, then back to head.)

Repeat Chorus (March in place throughout chorus.)

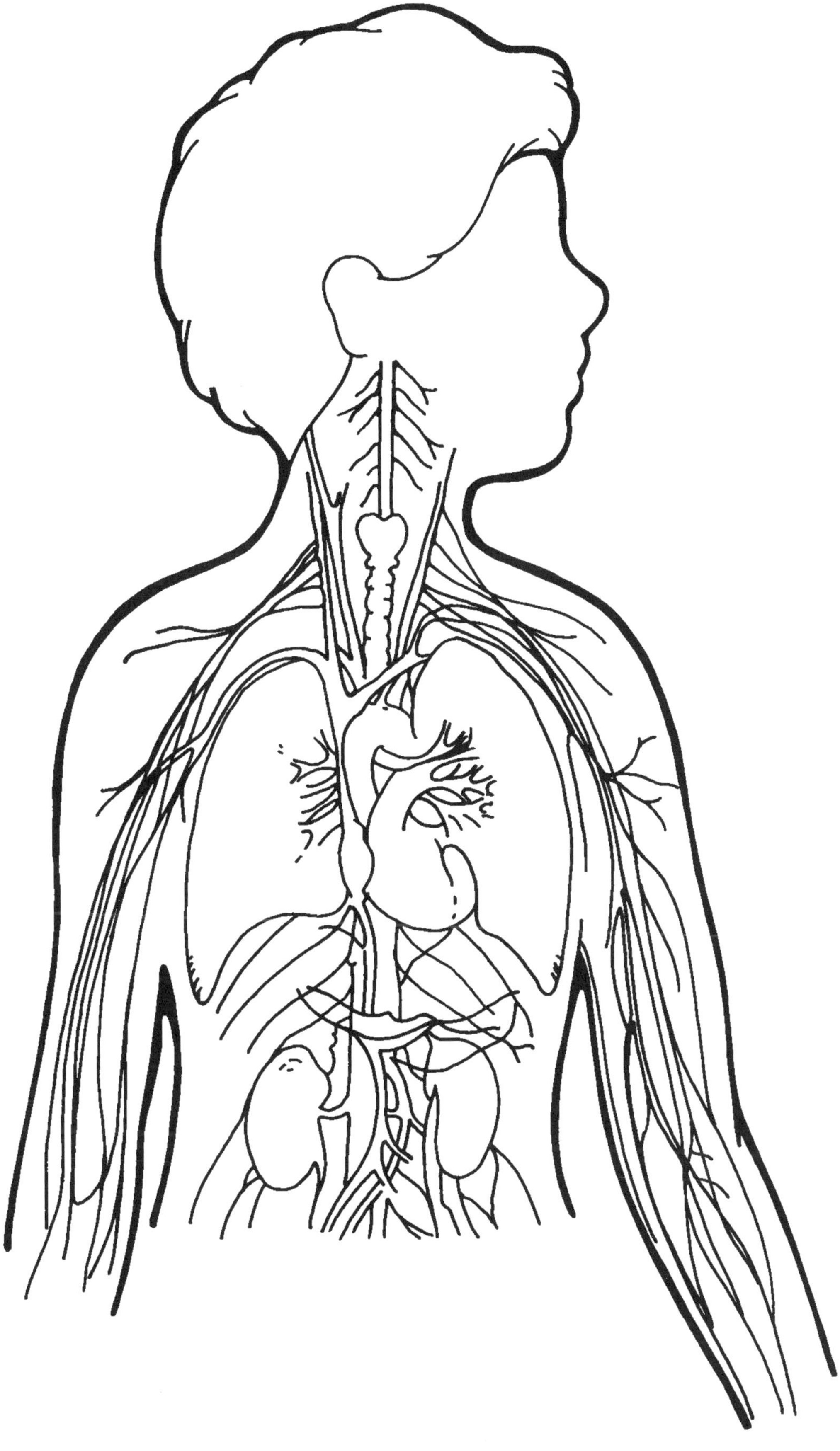

The Digestive System

"Oh Where, Oh Where Has My Little Dog Gone?" Tune

"Oh where, oh where has my pizza gone?"
My little brother came and asked me.
I told him the steps about digestion.
He listened, oh, so carefully!

It all starts by chewing the food in your mouth,
Yum, yum, it's now time to swallow.
Your esophagus takes your pizza on down,
It goes to your stomach below!

Your stomach's the place,
Where your food's broken down
By digestive juices you don't ever see.
Chemical changes will then take place,
Your stomach's one place where they'll be!

A liquid now forms in your small intestine,
It's filled with the food's nutrients.
They're absorbed by the blood
And fed to the cells.
It's starting to make perfect sense!

The parts of your food that you cannot digest
Move into your large intestine,
And soon leave your body as a waste.
Digestion has now taken place!

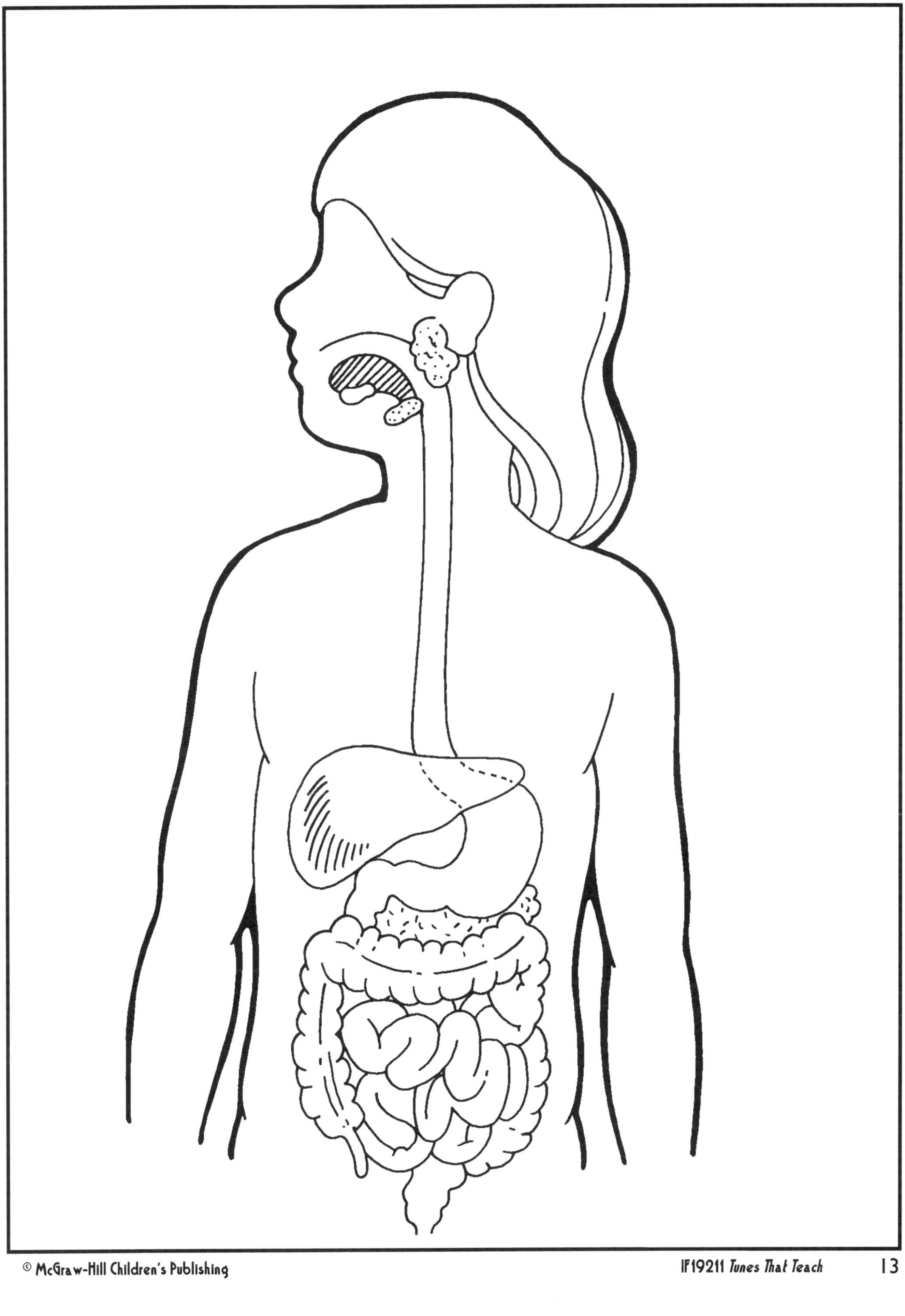

Disease Prevention

Tune "B-I-N-G-O"

There are small germs everywhere,
On doorknobs, hands, and in bathrooms.
G-E-R-M-S, G-E-R-M-S, G-E-R-M-S,
(Shake hands to beat of song.)
These germs are everywhere!

What can we do to not get sick?
We'll wash and scrub our hands!
S-C-R-U-B, S-C-R-U-B, S-C-R-U-B,
(Slide hands back and forth, palms together.)
We'll scrubs our hands together!

Germs may enter my body,
When someone coughs or sneezes,
C-O-V-E-R, C-O-V-E-R, C-O-V-E-R,
(Cup hands over mouth, alternating to beat.)
Cover your nose and mouth, please!

When we do things to not get sick,
We will stay real happy.
H-A-P-P-Y, H-A-P-P-Y, H-A-P-P-Y,
(Move pointer fingers up and down in air.)
We're happy and we're healthy!

Human Development and Relationships

Tune "London Bridge Is Falling Down"

Being friends is easy to do,
Easy to do,
And real fun, too!
Being friends is easy to do,
It's best for me and you!

We can show we care for all,
By being nice,
And sharing, too!
We can show we care for all,
By asking, "How are you?"

We can show respect for all,
By taking turns,
And helping, too!
We can show respect for all,
By saying "Please" and "Thank you!"

Identifying and Developing Our Talents

Tune: "My Bonnie Lies over the Ocean"

My talents are things that I work on,
My talents are things that help me,
Being a friend is just one kind, (Put arm around buddy.)
True friends are hard to find.

Chorus:
Listening helps me to be (Point to ear.)
The kind of friend that I like to see.
I make them smile and brighten their day!
Being a friend is a talent I say!

Playing the piano is another, (Pretend to play the piano.)
True talent that takes lots of time,
I practice and practice and practice,
It's one of my favorite pastimes.

Chorus:
Concentration is the key, (Point to head.)
Listening to teacher, so she'll help me.
Do my best and have lots of fun,
Learning notes and songs, one by one!

I have one more talent to share with you,
I love lots of sports can't you see. ("Swing" baseball bat in the air.)
But no matter which sport I am playing,
These are things which will help me!

Chorus:
Running, jumping, catching, swinging, (Run in place.)
All help this talent to grow and grow!
Follow the rules and be a good sport,
This is the end of my talent report!

My Many Talents

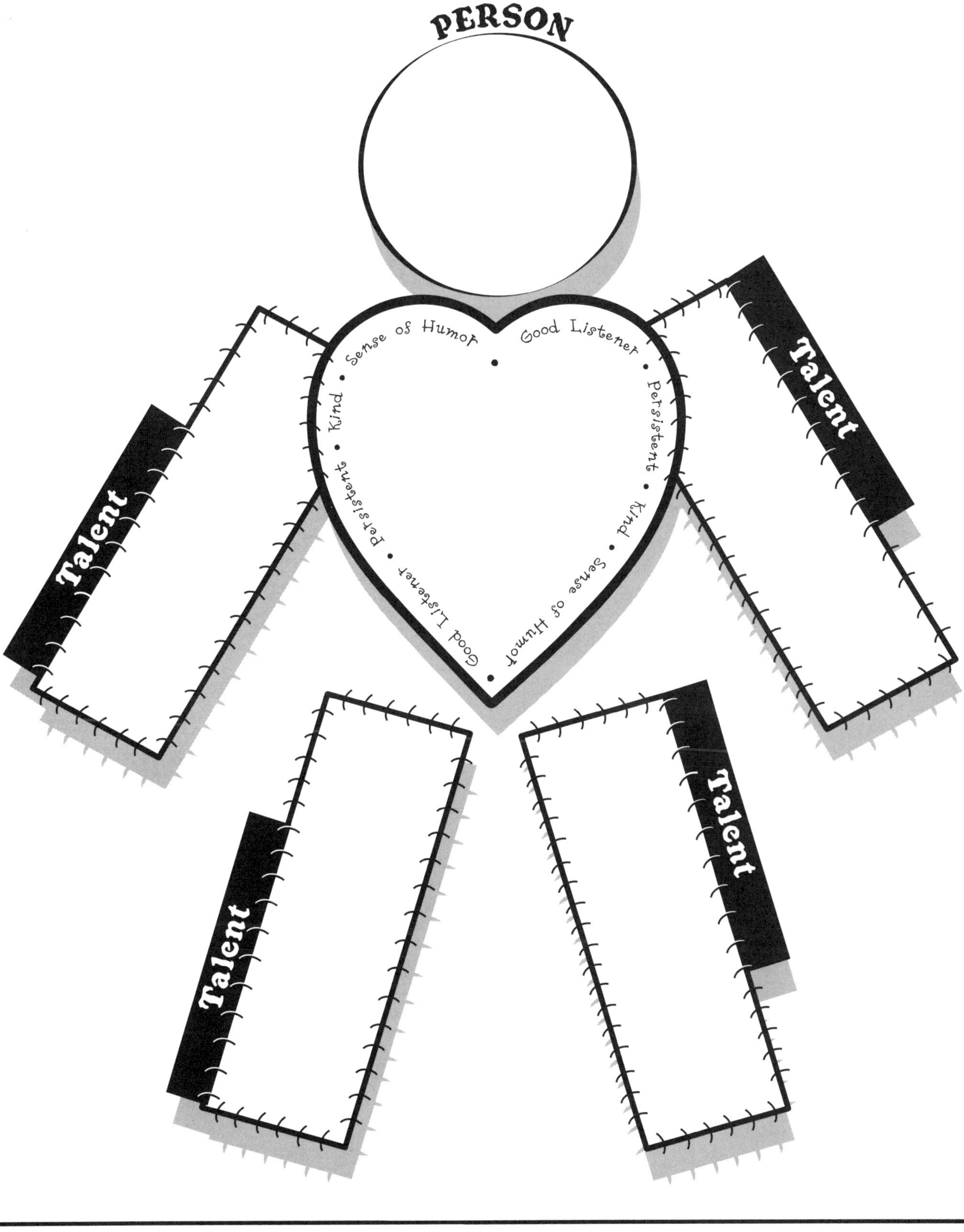

Mental and Physical Exercise

"Twinkle, Twinkle, Little Star" Tune

Exercise is really great! (Sway arms back and forth in running motion.)
It's my way to keep in shape!
Run or jump or dance or swim (Jump and make a swimmer's stroke motion.)
Keeps my body fit and slim.
Makes my muscles firm and strong (Flex muscles.)
So I'll live my life real long. (Put hands on hips.)

I can make my mind strong, too! (Put finger to head.)
Here are things that I can do.
Read good books or write a poem, (Open hands to form a book.)
Work in school and at my home.
Ask tough questions, be alert,
Think real hard, it doesn't hurt! (Point both fingers to each side of head.)

My Five Senses!

Tune "Mary Had a Little Lamb"

Yes, I have two eyes that see, eyes that see, eyes that see.
Yes, I have two eyes that see. The sense I use is SIGHT!

Yes, I use my nose to sniff, nose to sniff, nose to sniff.
Yes, I use my nose to sniff. The sense I use is SMELL!

Yes, I have two ears that hear, ears that hear, ears that hear.
Yes, I have two ears that hear. The sense I use is HEARING!

Yes, I use my tongue to taste, tongue to taste, tongue to taste.
Yes, I use my tongue to taste. The sense I use is TASTE!

Yes, I have two hands that feel, hands that feel, hands that feel.
Yes, I have two hands that feel. The sense I use is TOUCH!

These are called my five SENSES, five SENSES, five SENSES.
These are called my five SENSES. They're part of who I am!

My Five Senses!

by________

Things I can 

Things I can 

Things
I can

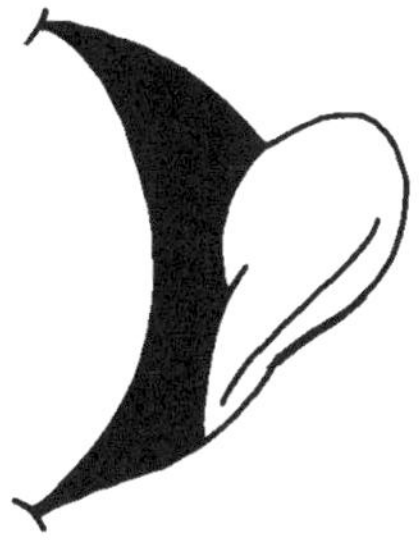

Things
I can

Things
I can

Resolving Conflict

"Oh! Susanna!" Tune

It was during recess, my friend and I,
We had a little fight.
He took my ball, and then ran off,
I knew it wasn't right!
I didn't know just what to do,
To the teacher, I ran.
She told me I could make a choice,
That's how it all began.

"She said!" (Say aloud without the tune.)

Chorus: Oh, dear (Michael)! (Choose a name.)
Go and find this friend!
Talk it over, and forgive him quick,
That's what I recommend!

During a test, my friend and I,
We were sitting side by side.
An answer she did not know,
Caused her wandering eye,
I didn't know just what to do,
But then remembered quick!
A little thing, my teacher said,
She shared a little trick!

"She said!" (Say aloud without the tune.)

Resolving Conflict, Cont.

Chorus: Oh, dear (Jenna)! (Choose a name.)
I'll talk to your friend.
We can study more, and feel real good,
That's what I recommend!

Our classmates may not all agree,
But that is not so bad,
We can solve our problems quickly,
This makes us not so mad.
Say, "I'm sorry" and then move on,
It's a good thing to do,
Look for solutions and then you'll see,
It's best for me and you!

Chorus: Solving problems
Can be an easy thing to do!
When you work together, it all pays off.
Your friends will do it, too!

The Skeletal System

"My Bonnie Lies over the Ocean" Tune

My body has a fantastic framework,
With two hundred and six strong white bones,
But inside they're soft and they're spongy,
They'll enlarge until I'm fully grown!

Chorus:
The skull and spine, hips and wrists,
Elbows and shoulder blades add to our lists.
Knees and ankles, ribs and toes,
Now for specific bones that I chose!

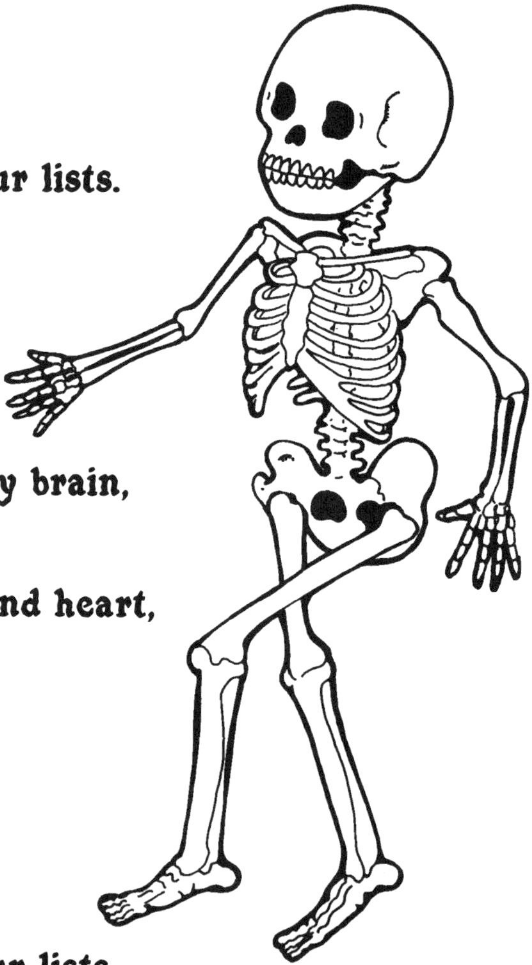

The bones in my skull will protect my brain,
Including my eyes and my ears,
My rib cage protects my soft lungs and heart,
My spine is my central support!

Chorus:
The skull and spine, hips and wrists,
Elbows and shoulder blades add to our lists.
Knees and ankles, ribs and toes,
It's time for this small song to close!

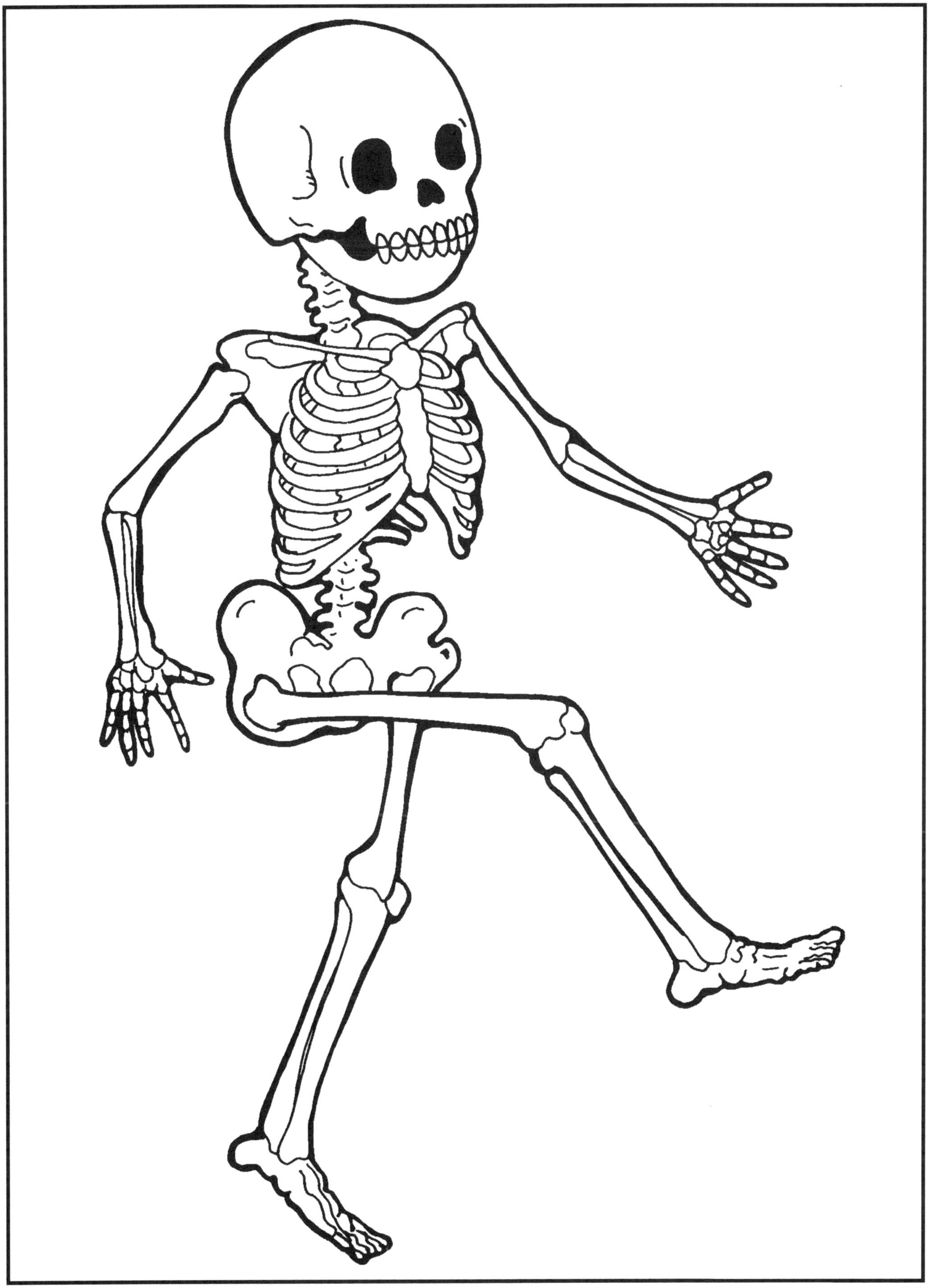

Stress Management

"Take Me Out to the Ball Game" Tune

I have a test that I'm worried about,
(Show worried look on face.)
An argument with my friend left me in doubt,
My heart's beating faster, my muscles tense up,
(Pat heart, feel muscles.)
My hands are sweaty. I'm too sick to get up.
(Shake hands, feel stomach.)
This thing's name is stress and I need a plan,
To help me feel better, and so I can stand.
(Point finger to the sky.)
Stress is the body's reaction to any demand,
To be ready–I'll relax beforehand!

I'll try not to worry and plan to be wise,
(Point finger to wristwatch.)
I'll study ahead and will be organized,
It will help to get plenty of rest and sleep,
(Close eyes, tilt head to side.)
I'll keep my room clean so it's not 20 feet deep,
My plan includes eating a diet that's right,
(Pretend to be eating.)
With exercise, I'll feel dynamite!
(Run in place.)
Now I've got my stress managed by me,
And it's better, GUARANTEED!
(March in place triumphantly.)

Teacher Tips and Suggestions

for Language Arts Tunes

Days of the Week/Months of the Year (Page 29)

Using the "Army Cadence Chant," these songs can be sung in a variety of ways. You, as the teacher, could chant each line, having your students respond with the echo. Alternately, you could ask one student to act as the "drill sergeant" while other members of the class echo each line. The class could also be divided into two sections with each side taking turns leading or being the echo. No matter which variation you use, be sure to march in place while chanting this tune!

Fact and Opinion (Page 30)

After the students sing the verse on facts, pause in the song and call on different students to shout out different facts. For example, one might say, "It is 95 degrees outside today." Follow the same procedure after singing the verse about opinions. One might say, "It is a beautiful day." What a fun way to practice the difference between fact and opinion!

Hard and Soft "C" and "G" (Page 31)

On the second line of each verse, be sure to make the sound of the letter instead of saying the actual letter name. Also, after the lines that say, "Look for other words around!" have different students shout out words with the sound previously mentioned in that verse. For example, after the first verse, students can shout out words like: clock, cup, cake, candy, coat, and cat. Some "S" sounds for the letter "C" include: pencil, face, celery, and mice. Some words with the hard "G" sound include: game, gum, egg, goose, and gift. Some words with the "J" sound for the letter "G" include: giraffe, giant, stage, and cage.

Long Vowels with an "E" at the End (Page 32)

Write examples of words mentioned in the song on the chalkboard. While singing, underline the first vowel as it corresponds with the song. When you sing the line "it disappears so quietly," erase the end "e" in the word on the board.

Sequence of Events (Page 33)

Relate personal examples using the key words. Invite the students to come up with their own stories using these key words. Here is an example: "First I woke up this morning. Next I brushed my teeth. Then I got dressed. Finally I ate breakfast. At last I rode the bus to school." Students also may be encouraged to complete each line of a sequence! For example, they can write the main steps for making chocolate chip cookies.

Teacher Tips and Suggestions, Cont.

Two Vowels Together in a Word (Page 34)

After each line that says, "The first is in charge of the other!" pause during the song to write down examples of the same rule previously mentioned in that verse. Students can also call out examples that apply to that rule.

Examples after the first verse: boat, soap, coat
Examples after the second verse: sail, pail, wail, nail, jail
Examples after the third verse: tie, lie
Examples after the fourth verse: dream, team, beagle

Tip: Draw, color, and cut out an "in charge" character (whatever you would like it to be). As you sing the song, write the words on the board. Place this character above the vowel in the word that is "in charge," meaning it is the sound you hear in the word.

"Y" as a Vowel (Page 35)

After each line that says, "Let's try some more today!" pause in the song to write other examples of the same rule previously mentioned in that verse. Students can also call out examples that apply to that rule.

"Y" that sounds like "I" in words:
my, myself, why, try, lying, shy
"Y" that sounds like "E" in words:
happy, greatly, suddenly, finally, wimpy

Days of the Week

Tune "Army Cadence Chant"

I don't know, but I've been told, (Repeat as echo.)
The days of the week are as good as gold! (Repeat as echo.)
Sunday, Monday, Tuesday, Wednesday, too! (Repeat as echo.)
Thursday, Friday, Saturday, all week through! (Repeat as echo.)

Sound off! (Sunday! Monday!)
A little bit more! (Tuesday! Wednesday!)
Thursday, Friday, Saturday! (HOORAY!)

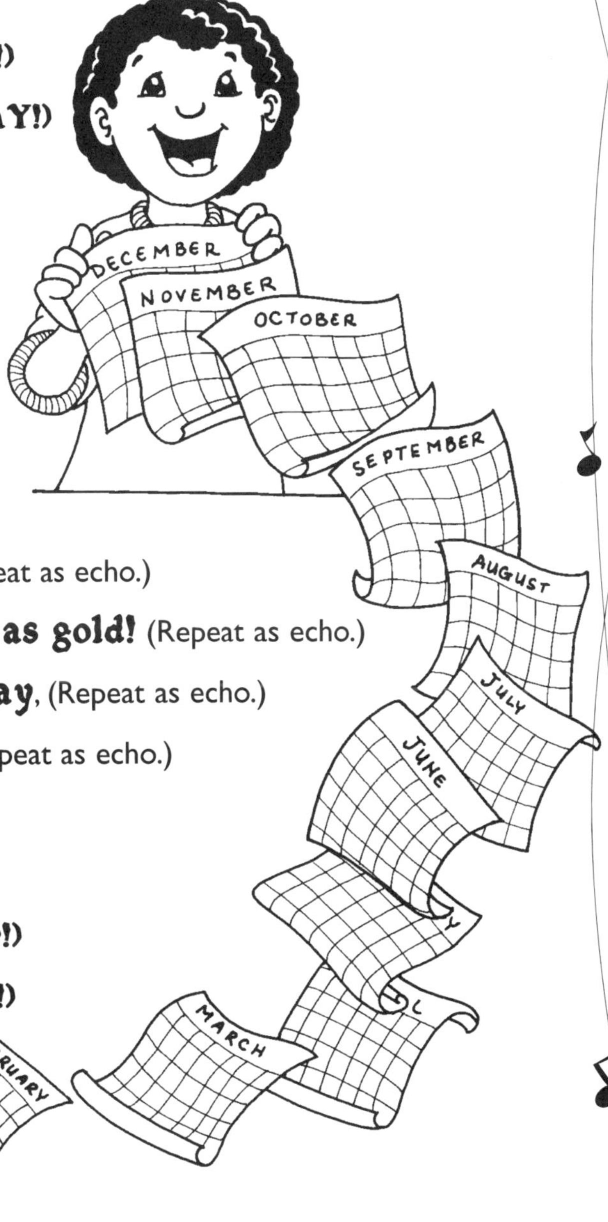

Months of the Year

Tune: "Army Cadence Chant"

I don't know, but I've been told, (Repeat as echo.)
The months of the year are as good as gold! (Repeat as echo.)
January, February, March, April, May, (Repeat as echo.)
June, July, August is what I say! (Repeat as echo.)

Sound off! (September! October!)
A little bit more! (November! December!)
There are 12 months. (And NO MORE!)

Fact and Opinion

"Skip to My Lou" Tune

Facts, facts, facts can be proven,
They are events that really happened!
Facts, facts, facts can be proven.
Here's an example of a fact:

The pyramids are located in Egypt.

Opinions are what you think,
What you believe, or how you feel!
Opinions are what you think.
Here's an example of opinion:

I think the trees are beautiful.

Hard and Soft "C" and "G"

Tune "Row, Row, Row Your Boat"

C, C, C can make a hard or soft sound,
Hard is "K" and soft is "S."
Look for other words around!

C, C, C can make a hard or soft sound,
Hard is "K" and soft is "S."
Look for other words around!

G, G, G can make a hard or soft sound,
Hard is "G" and soft is "J."
Look for other words around!

G, G, G can make a hard or soft sound,
Hard is "G" and soft is "J."
Look for other words around!

Long Vowels with an "E" at the End

Tune
"Old MacDonald Had a Farm"

An "E" at the end, makes the first vowel say
Its very, very own name,
Like "A" in cake and "A" in lake,
And "A" in made and game.

You don't hear the "E," it's as silent as can be
It disappears so quietly!
An "E" at the end makes the first vowel say,
Its very, very own name!

An "E" at the end, makes the first vowel say
Its very, very own name,
Like "I" in dime and "I" in time,
And "I" in kite and like.

You don't hear the "E," it's as silent as can be,
It disappears so quietly!
An "E" at the end makes the first vowel say
It's very, very own name!

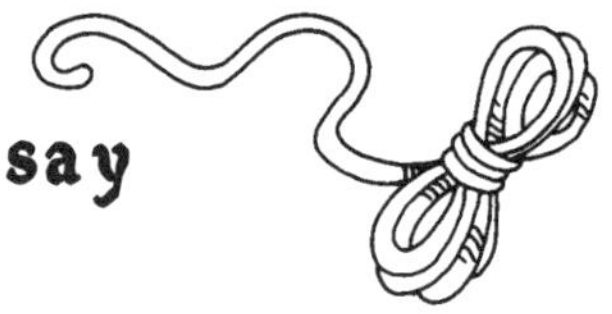

An "E" at the end makes the first vowel say
Its very, very own name,
Like "O" in note and "O" in rope,
And "O" in nose and hope.

You don't hear the "E," it's as silent as can be,
It disappears so quietly!
An "E" at the end makes the first vowel say
Its very, very own name!

An "E" at the end makes the first vowel say
Its very, very own name.
Like "U" in tune and "U" in June,
And "U" in blue and cute.

You don't hear the "E," it's as silent as can be,
It disappears so quietly!
An "E" at the end makes the first vowel say
Its very, very own name!

Sequence of Events

Tune: "Frère Jacques"

Telling a story
Is quite simple
If you know
The sequence of events.
There are clues that tell you
The order that things happen,
First, next, then,
Finally, at last.

I'll tell you an example
of how these words happen–
First, next, then,
Finally, at last.
Then you, too, can do it
and understand sequence.
Here we go,
A sequence of events!

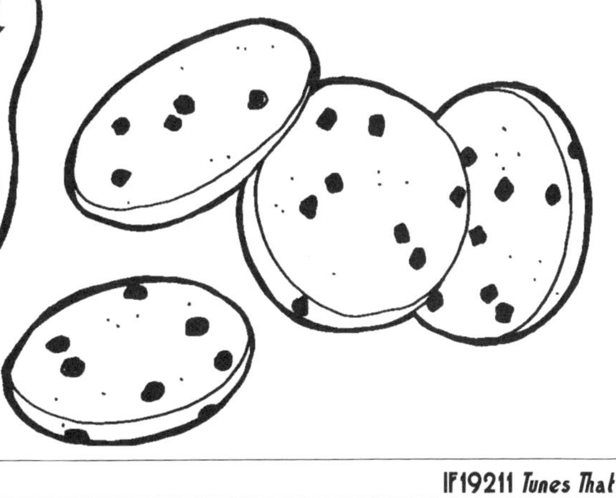

Two Vowels Together in a Word

Tune "Oh, Where Has My Little Dog Gone?"

Oh where, oh where has that little "A" gone?
In "goat," it was after the "O."
It's because when two vowels are close together,
The first is in charge of the other!

Oh where, oh where has that little "I" gone?
In "mail," it was after the "A."
It's because when two vowels are close together,
The first is in charge of the other!

Oh where, oh where has that little "E" gone?
In "pie," it was after the "I."
It's because when two vowels are close together,
The first is in charge of the other!

Oh where, oh where has that little "A" gone?
In "eagle," it was after the "E."
It's because when two vowels are close together,
The first is in charge of the other!

"Y" as a Vowel

Tune "Row, Row, Row Your Boat"

A-E-I-O-U are vowels that we all know,
But "Y" can be a vowel, too,
As I will now show!

The letter "Y" can sound like "I"
In words we say each day,
"Dry" and "sky," "cry" and "fly,"
Let's try some more today!

The letter "Y" can sound like "E"
In words we say each day,
"Baby," "bunny," "pony," "puppy,"
Let's try some more today!

Teacher Tips and Suggestions

for Math Tunes

Addition and Subtraction (Page 38)

Prior to singing, write the words "sum," "plus," "all together," "minus," "difference," and "How many more?" onseparate pieces of tagboard. Ask six students to come to the front of the room and hold the cards. When a particular word or phrase is being sung, a student should hold up the corresponding sign. When the words "addition" or "subtraction" are sung, students in class can model the signs. Show the addition sign by crossing your arms in front of yourself. Show the subtraction sign by placing one arm horizontally in front of self.

Cool Geometry! (Page 39)

Follow each action as directed on the song page. Point out other examples of these terms found in the classroom.

Counting by 2s, Counting by 5s (Page 41)

Lead students in skipping around the room while singing this upbeat tune. Children can take turns being the leader.

Geometry in Our World (Page 42)

Have the children point to different objects in the classroom or outside as they sing the chorus. They'll love it!

Geometry–Space Figures (Page 43)

Bring examples of these space figures to class. Hold them up while singing the song. As a follow-up activity, play a "Geometry Memory Match" game. Photocopy the pattern pages (see pages 44 and 45) onto heavy paper and then cut apart the cards. Color as desired. Tape them *facedown* on the chalkboard. Have the students try to match the space figure (geometric solid) with its common object. Each student selects two cards and turns them *faceup*. If a match is made, the student collects the cards. If a match is not made, the student turns the cards *facedown* again. Students continue taking turns until all matches are found. Another activity idea: make a geometry scavenger hunt worksheet for students to list/draw other examples of these geometric shapes found in their homes or school environment.

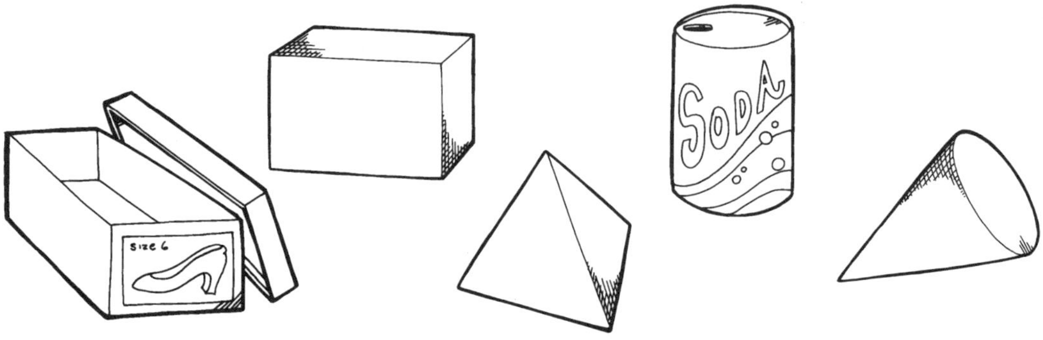

Identifying Two-Digit Numbers (Page 46)

Ask different children to call out a number while the class joins in by singing the answer. For another variation, print the words "ones" and "tens" on tagboard cards. Also print the numerals 0–9 on large pieces of tagboard. Display the place value cards on a board. Pass out the number cards to your students. When a number is mentioned in the song, the students who hold the corresponding numeral cards can move quickly to the board and place the cards in the correct place value columns.

Odd and Even Numbers (Page 47)

Ask for two students to hold hands together in the air forming a bridge. Play is similar to the game "London Bridge Is Falling Down." Children pass under the bridge until everyone sings, "20." When "20" is sung, the "bridge" comes down and captures the student who is under it. Those holding the "bridge" sway the student gently back and forth while singing, "These are even numbers, from 2 through 20!" The same idea applies to the verse on the odd numbers. The "bridge" comes down when students sing, "19."

Time (Page 47)

Display a clock and a calendar. Using these two objects, demonstrate the concepts that are outlined in the song. Be sure to have everyone march while singing this fun song. Students can take turns being the lead singer while others respond with the echo part. If appropriate, encourage your students to solve various math problems by using their calculators. For example, "If there are 24 hours in one day, how many hours are in two days?" Students can then add 24 plus 24 or multiply 24 by 2, depending on their skill levels.

The Value of Coins (Page 48)

Students shout out the answers to fill in the blanks. Select either U.S. or Canadian coins. Copy, color, cut out, and laminate the coins on pattern page 49. Have the students hold up the corresponding cards while singing the song.

Zero in Addition and Subtraction (Page 50)

Write examples on the board that are found in the song. Challenge your students to list even more examples. Use manipulatives to illustrate this concept. For example, if the problem is "3 + 0," take out three math counters and "add" zero additional pieces. What do you have? Of course, it is the same number with which you started! You may want to let the students try some examples of their own with a partner.

Addition and Subtraction

Tune: "I've Been Working on the Railroad"

I've been working on addition,
All the day long through.
Yes, I've been working on addition
And have found out a couple of clues!

When I hear the words "sum" or "plus,"
Addition is what I'll do!
"All together" means the same thing,
Addition works here, too!

I've been working on subtraction,
All the day long through.
Yes, I've been working on subtraction,
And have found out it's easy to do!

When someone asks, "How many more?"
Subtraction is what I'll do!
"Minus" and "difference" mean the same thing,
Subtraction works here, too!

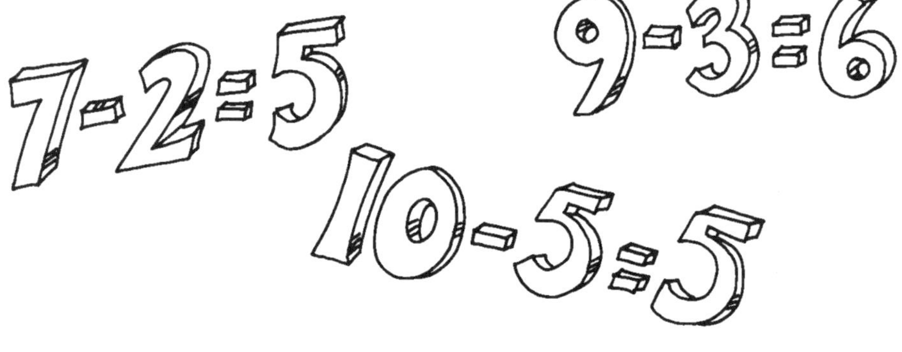

Cool Geometry! (Lines, Line Segments, Parallel, Intersecting, & Angles)

Tune "The Ants Go Marching"

A line goes on in both directions,
(Extend arms out to each side, palms down.)

Hooray, hooray.
(Pump both arms high in the air.)

A line goes on in both directions,
(Extend arms out to each side, palms down.)

Hooray, hooray.
(Pump both arms high in the air.)

A line goes on in both directions,
(Extend arms out to each side, palms down.)

But a line segment stops on the dots!
(Put both arms in front of self/hands in fists.)

And they all are part of cool geometry!
(Fan face with hands.)

Boom, boom, boom!
(Clap hands three times.)

Parallel lines look like tracks,
(Extend both arms in front of self.)

Hooray, hooray.
(Pump both arms high in the air.)

Parallel lines look like tracks,
(Extend both arms in front of self.)

Hooray, hooray.
(Pump both arms high in the air.)

Cool Geometry! Cont.

Parallel lines look like tracks,
(Extend both arms in front of self.)

And never do they intersect,
(Shake head, cross extended arms in front of self.)

And they all are part of cool geometry!
(Fan face with hands.)

Boom, boom, boom!
(Clap hands three times.)

A true right angle is 90 degrees,
(Raise right arm to right ear, extend left arm out.)

Hooray, hooray.
(Pump both arms high in the air.)

A true right angle is 90 degrees,
(Raise right arm to right ear, extend left arm out.)

Hooray, hooray.
(Pump both arms high in the air.)

A true right angle is 90 degrees,
(Raise right arm to right ear, extend left arm out.)

But obtuse is more and acute is less,
(Keep left arm out, move right arm out to make an obtuse angle. Then bring arms back to form an acute angle.)

And they all are part of cool geometry!
(Fan face with hands.)

Boom, boom, boom, BOOM!

Counting by 2s, Counting by 5s

Tune "The Farmer in the Dell"

When I go out to play
During the day,
I slide my feet and give a hop,
(Slide to one side, hop once.)
Skipping! Oh, hooray!

I can do the same,
When counting in my brain!
(Point to head.)
I skip some numbers two by two,
(Raise two fingers in air.)
It's so EASY to do!

Chant:
2, 4, 6, 8, 10, 12, 14, 16, 18,
20, 22, 24, 26, 28, and now 30!

Fives are not so bad,
I can do them in my head!
(Raise five fingers in air.)
By adding five to the number before,
Now I'm ready for more!

Chant:
5, 10, 15, 20, 25 and 30,
35 and 40 now, 45 and 50!

Math

Geometry in Our World

Tune: "My Bonnie Lies over the Ocean"

There's all sorts of shapes all around me,
Triangles, circles, and squares!
Each one is so very different!
Try to name some, if you dare!

"O.K.!" (Say aloud without the tune.)

Chorus:
Over there!
Everywhere!
I see a circle, and then a square!
Ooohh! Some more!
The ball, cone, and door!
There are shapes all around to explore!

Geometry — Space Figures

Tune "Take Me Out to the Ball Game"

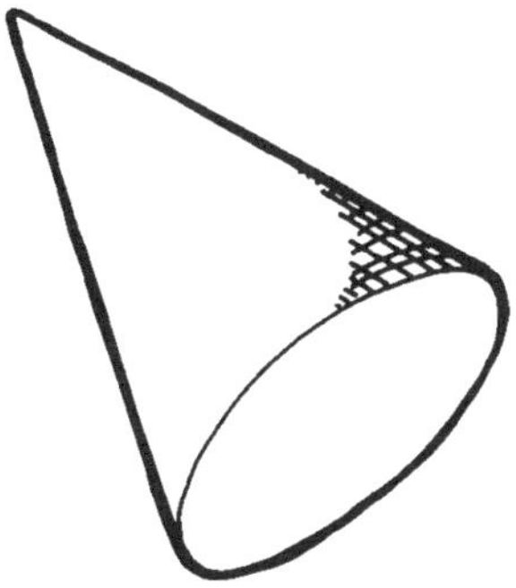

There are some figures that take up space,
We like to say they're "3-D,"
Rectangular prisms or cylinders,
Cubes and cones, spheres and great pyramids!
Now to show how they're all worthwhile,
They're really quite easy to find.
Look around, they're taking up space,
In this big world of yours and mine!

"For instance!" (Say aloud without the tune.)

Rectangular prisms are like a shoe box,
Spheres, a round basketball,
Cubes like ice cubes, and then there's cones
For holding good ice cream, that's all my own!
Pyramids as in Egypt, cylinders as in cans,
Now you see these things every day,
Geometry's here to stay!

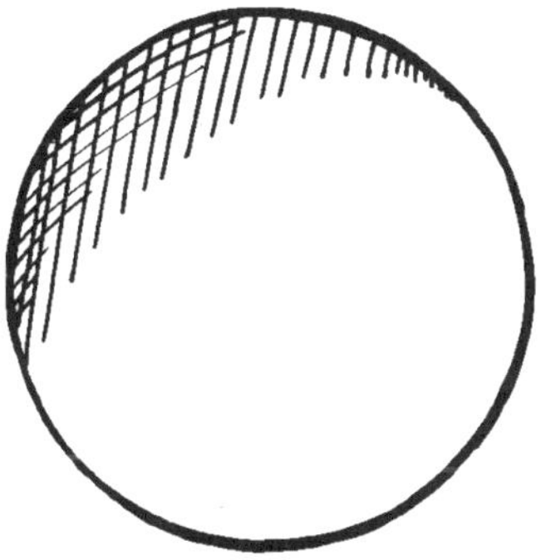

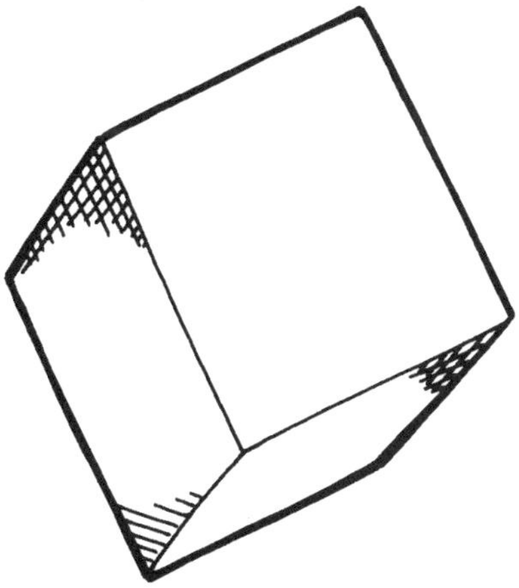

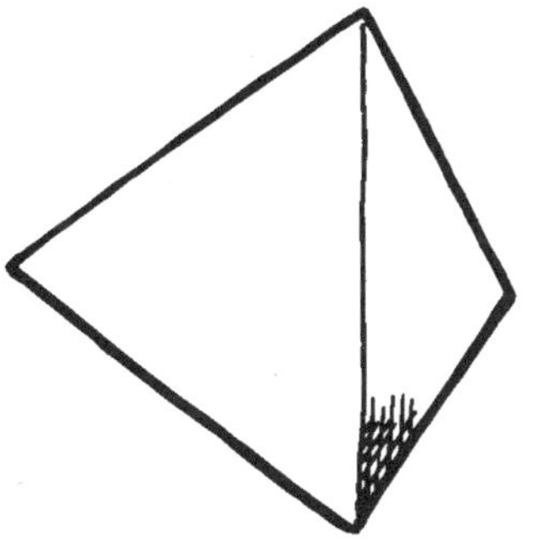

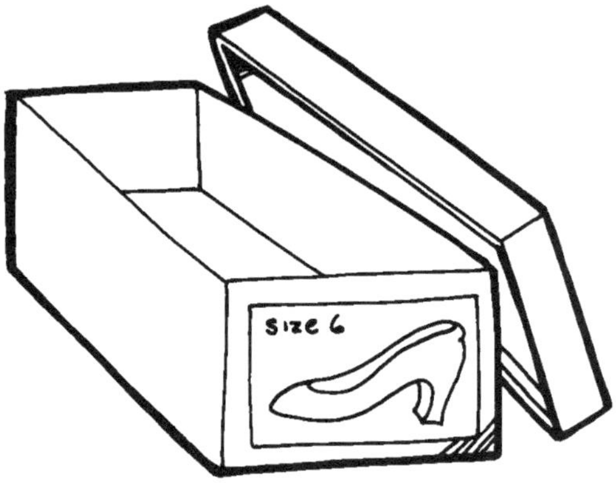
size 6

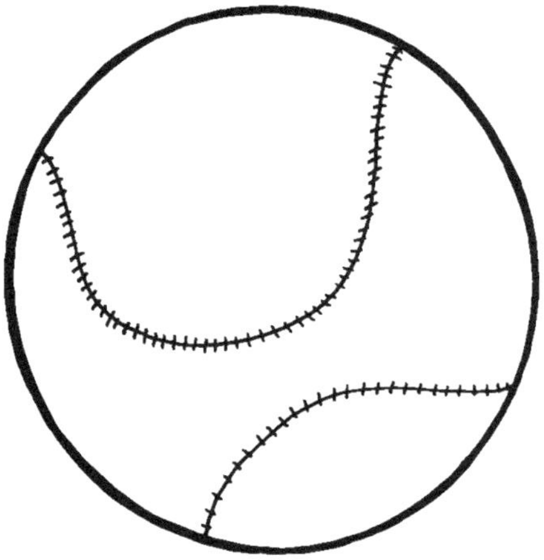

SODA

Snow
Cone

Picture Cards for "Space Figures"

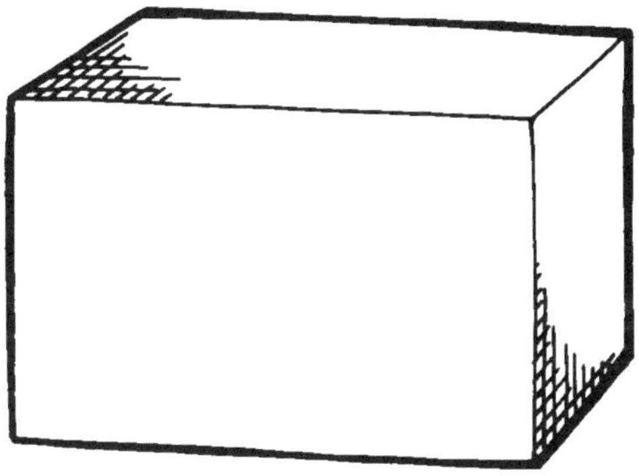

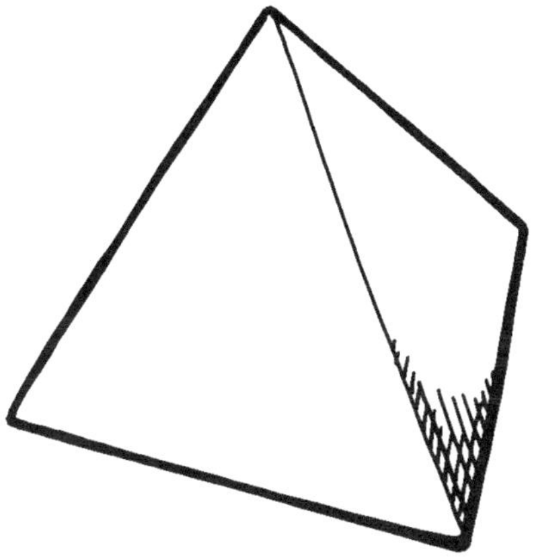

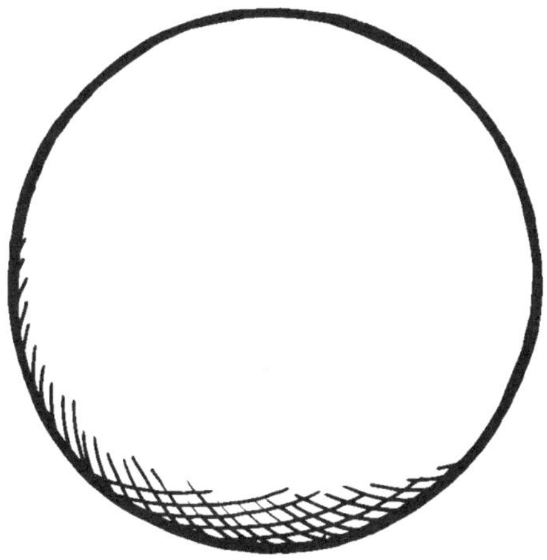

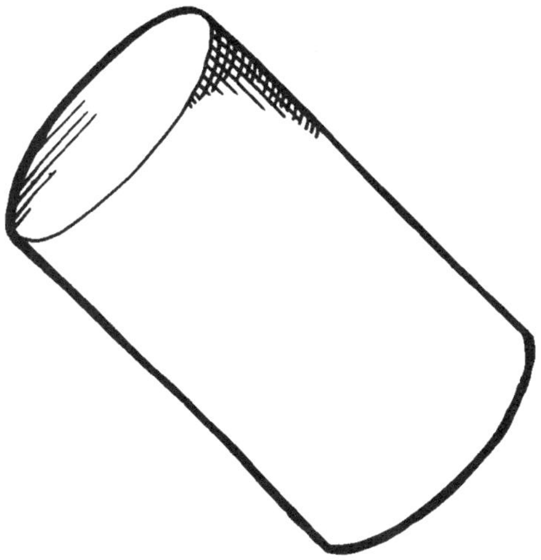

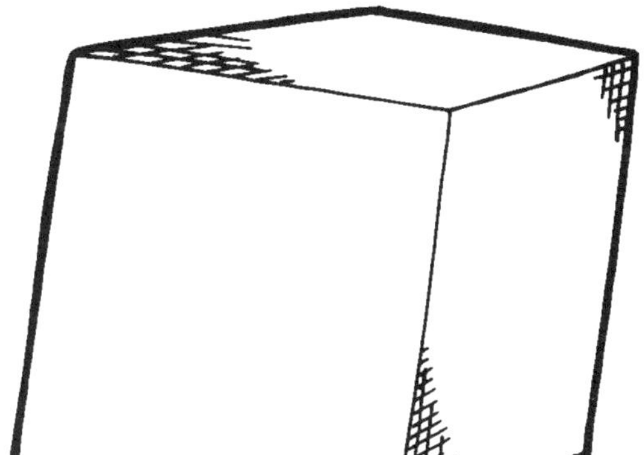

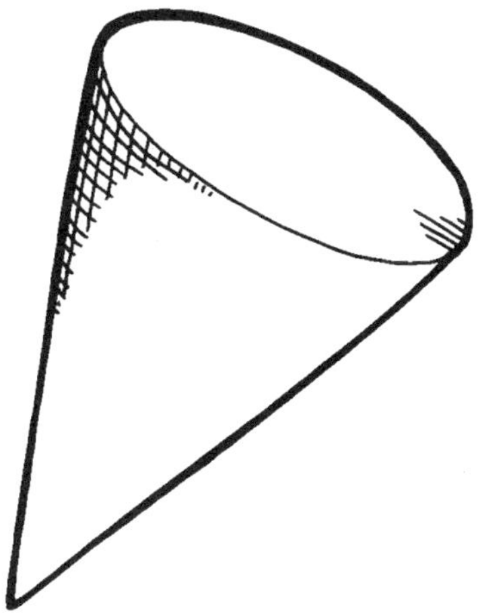

Identifying Two-Digit Numbers

Tune: "Skip to My Lou"

Chorus:
Numbers have places, yes, they do,
Numbers have places, yes, they do,
Numbers have places, yes, they do,
Ones' and tens' places tried and true!

12 is the number, what are the places?
12 is the number, what are the places?
12 is the number, what are the places?
2's in the ones' place, 1 in the tens'!

Repeat Chorus

35's the number, what are the places?
35's the number, what are the places?
35's the number, what are the places?
5's in the ones' place, 3's in the tens'!

Repeat Chorus

58's the number, what are the places?
58's the number, what are the places?
58's the number, what are the places?
8's in the ones' place, 5's in the tens'!

Repeat Chorus

Odd and Even Numbers

Tune "London Bridge Is Falling Down"

2, 4, 6, 8, 10, 12, 14,
16, 18, then there's 20!
These are even numbers,
from 2 through 20!

1, 3, 5, 7, 9, 11, 13,
15, 17, then there's 19!
These numbers are all odd,
1 through 19!

Time

Tune: "Army Cadence Chant"

I don't know but I've been told! (Repeat as echo.)
I am just one minute old! (Repeat as echo.)
Sixty seconds have gone by! (Repeat as echo.)
My, oh my, how time does fly! (Repeat as echo.)
Count off! (Sixty seconds!) That makes! (Just one minute!)
Sixty seconds . . . in one minute!

I don't know but I've been told! (Repeat as echo.)
I am just one hour old! (Repeat as echo.)
Sixty minutes have gone by! Repeat as echo.)
My, oh my, how time does fly! (Repeat as echo.)
Count off! (60 minutes!) That makes! (Just one hour!)
Sixty minutes . . . in one hour!

Use echo after each phrase except as indicated:

I don't know but I've been told! I am just one day old!
Twenty-four hours have gone by! My, oh my, how time does fly!
Count off! (24 hours!) That makes! (Just one day!)
Twenty-four hours . . . in one day!

Math

The Value of Coins

Tune: "She'll Be Comin' 'Round the Mountain"

I hear the jingle, jingle, jingle in my pocket!
I'm so happy I have money for my rocket!
Now I need to count the change, so I can prearrange,
How much each coin is worth in my pocket!

Now each penny equals only just one cent!
That's the smallest part of what I plan to spend!
Every nickel equals five and a dime equals ten,
My quarter is just twenty-five more cents!

Now it's time for a little review,
I understand my money, how about you?
A penny equals ______, a nickel equals ______,
My dime is ______, my quarter's ________!

IN GOD WE TRUST
LIBERTY
2001
UNITED STATES OF AMERICA
E PLURIBUS UNUM
ONE CENT

IN GOD WE TRUST
LIBERTY
2001
E PLURIBUS UNUM
MONTICELLO
FIVE CENTS
UNITED STATES OF AMERICA

LIBERTY
2001
UNITED STATES OF AMERICA
ONE DIME

LIBERTY
IN GOD WE TRUST
2001
UNITED STATES OF AMERICA
E PLURIBUS UNUM
QUARTER DOLLAR

ELIZABETH II
D·G·REGINA
1 CENT
CANADA

ELIZABETH II
D·G·REGINA
5 CENTS
CANADA
1990

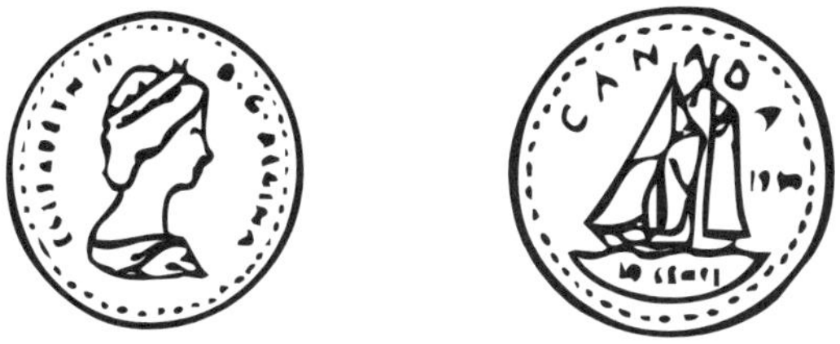
CANADA

ELIZABETH II
D·G·REGINA
CANADA
25 cents

Zero in Addition and Subtraction

Tune: "The Farmer in the Dell"

When I'm trying to add or subtract with a zero,
It's easy because the number's the same,
And now I'm a math pro!

Three plus zero is three, three minus zero is three,
A million plus zero is still a million,
You can see it's so easy!

Ten plus zero is ten, ten minus zero is ten,
A million minus zero is still a million,
I'll sing it once again!

When I'm trying to add, or subtract with a zero,
It's easy because the number's the same,
And now I'm a math pro!

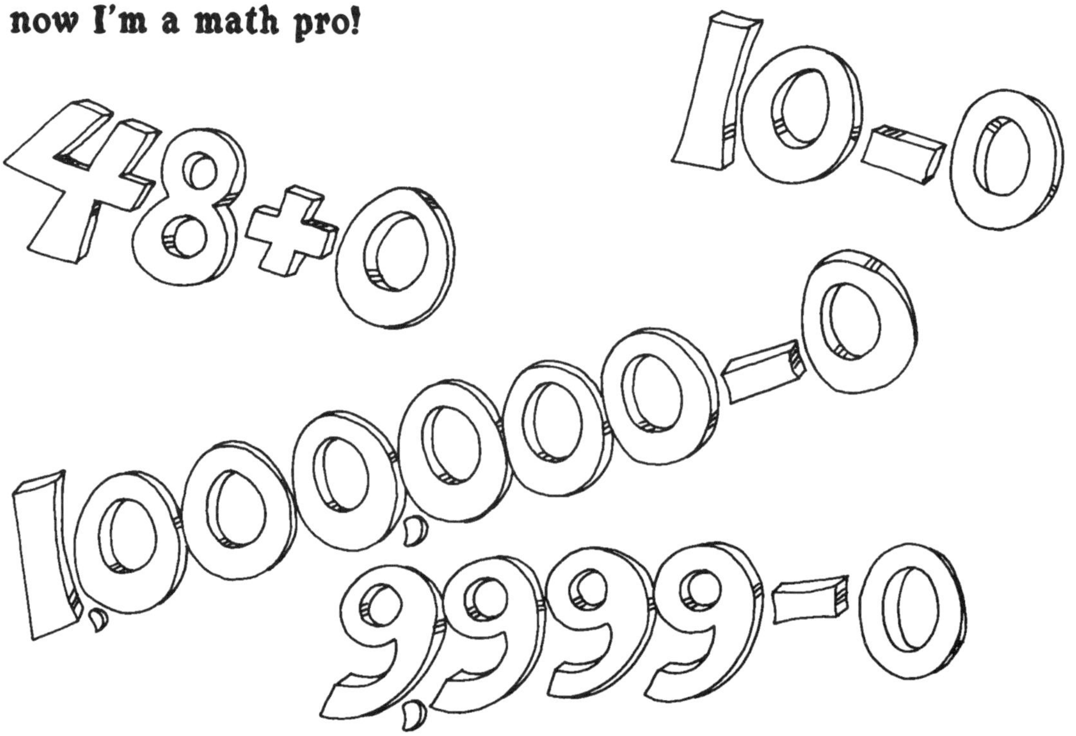

Teacher Tips and Suggestions

for Science Tunes

Air (Page 53)

Follow each action as instructed on the song page.

Animal Variations and Animal Body Coverings (Page 54)

Lyrics for "Animal Body Coverings" can be sung as a round immediately after the first line. As a follow-up activity, reproduce pattern page 55 for the children to make an animal booklet that follows the lyrics of the song. Children can fill in the blanks or recite while an adult records their answers in their booklets. Have the children illustrate and cut apart the pages. Staple them together to make their new mini-books!

Continents and Oceans (Page 56)

Using a pointer stick, point to the different continents and oceans on a large map while singing the song. For fun, increase the tempo each time and see how fast your students can point to the corresponding continent or ocean!

Electrical Safety (Page 57)

Copy pattern page 58 onto an overhead transparency. Use the overhead projector to display the pictures of Carmen and Doug while singing the song. Discuss how to handle electrical tools and appliances safely. Afterwards, display a copy of the pictures in the room as a reminder to the students of electrical safety.

Erosion (Page 59)

Bring a large rock to class. Have the students stand in a circle, passing the rock around while singing the song. When the song ends on its final note, the person who has the rock in his/her hand moves to the center of the circle. Perhaps the winner could receive some rock candy!

Fossils (Page 60)

Tip: Speed up lines 5–8 and lines 13–16.

Habitats and Food Chains (Page 61)

A perfect song for singing in a round!

Light (Page 62)

Prepare students for the concepts of light mentioned in the song by having them experiment with prisms, flashlights, and mirrors.

Teacher Tips and Suggestions, Cont.

Magnets (Page 63)

Carry a big magnet around the room while the students are singing and try to pick up objects. Children would love to have a turn at this, too!

Mammals (Page 64)

March in line and act like the animals! Make individual copies of the "Mammals" booklet (see pages 65–66) following the song. Students can illustrate the pages. There are three blank pages at the end of the booklet to feature additional mammals that are being studied.

Matter (Page 67)

Conduct some simple science investigations to learn about the three states of matter.

Seasons (Page 68)

Copy "The Sensational Seasons" booklet (see pages 69–73) for each student to make. Your young artists may enjoy illustrating the scenes for this song.

Shadows (Page 74)

Take the children on a walk outside. Sing the song as they make shadows along the sidewalk. Be sure to observe shadows at different times of the day to notice how they change.

Simple Machines (Page 75)

Provide copies of page 76 for the students. Have the students look through magazines or catalogs, clip examples of these simple machines, and glue them onto their cards. *Tip:* Do not try to sing all of the verses at once. This song works best when taught over several sessions.

Taking a Raindrop Through the Water Cycle (Page 77)

Make a large raindrop on construction paper for each student in class to color and cut out. During the song, have the students pretend their raindrops are moving through the water cycle.

Water, The Water Cycle, and More About the Water Cycle! (Page 78)

All three of these songs can be sung in rounds. Have the students draw pictures to show the four stages of the water cycle. Display the pictures when singing these songs.

Tools to Measure and Predict Weather (Page 79)

Show actual tools for measuring weather or provide copies of pattern page 80 to display when singing the song. Ask students to hold up the corresponding tool/picture at the appropriate times. Then mix up the order of the tools and sing the song again. This will give the students more practice to identify the tools correctly.

Air

Tune "For He's a Jolly Good Fellow"

Oh, you cannot see the air,	(Point to eyes.)
You cannot smell the air,	(Point to nose.)
You cannot taste the air,	(Point to mouth.)
But air is here and there!	(Extend left arm, then right arm.)

Chorus:

The air is here and there!	(Extend left arm, then right arm.)
The air is here and there!	(Extend left arm, then right arm.)

It has to take up the space,	(Swing arm out in front of self.)
All around the place,	
We need it to live and grow,	(Raise arms toward sky.)
And that you ought to know!	(Point to head.)

Repeat Chorus

And wind is moving air,	(Sway back and forth.)
We feel it through our hair,	(Feel through hair.)
We take it into our lungs,	(Take deep breath in.)
And that's our little song!	(Clap three times.)

Repeat Chorus

Animal Variations

Tune: "She'll Be Comin' 'Round the Mountain"

Animals need food and water! Yes, they do!
Air and shelter are greatly needed, too!
Air and shelter, food and water,
Are things that really matter,
They tell the animals "We care about you!"

Animal Body Coverings

Tune: "Frère Jacques"

We wear clothes
To keep warm.
How do animals
Do the same?
Feathers are on birds,
Scales are on fish,
Fur on mammals,
Fur on mammals.

I ♡ Animals and Animals ♡ ME!

By ________ 1

I eat ____________ . 2

Animals eat ________ . 3

I live in a ________ . 4

Animals live in a

______________ . 5

I wear a __________

to keep warm. 6

Animals wear

____

to keep warm. 7

I love

animals . . . 8

. . . and animals

love me! 9

Continents and Oceans

Tune "Three Blind Mice"

Seven masses of land,
Each a continent.
Find them on a globe.
It's time well spent.
North and South America,
Africa and Asia,
Europe and Antarctica,
And Australia!

Four bodies of water,
Each an ocean.
Find them on a globe.
It's really quite fun.
Atlantic and Pacific,
Then there's Indian,
Don't forget the Arctic,
And now you're all done!

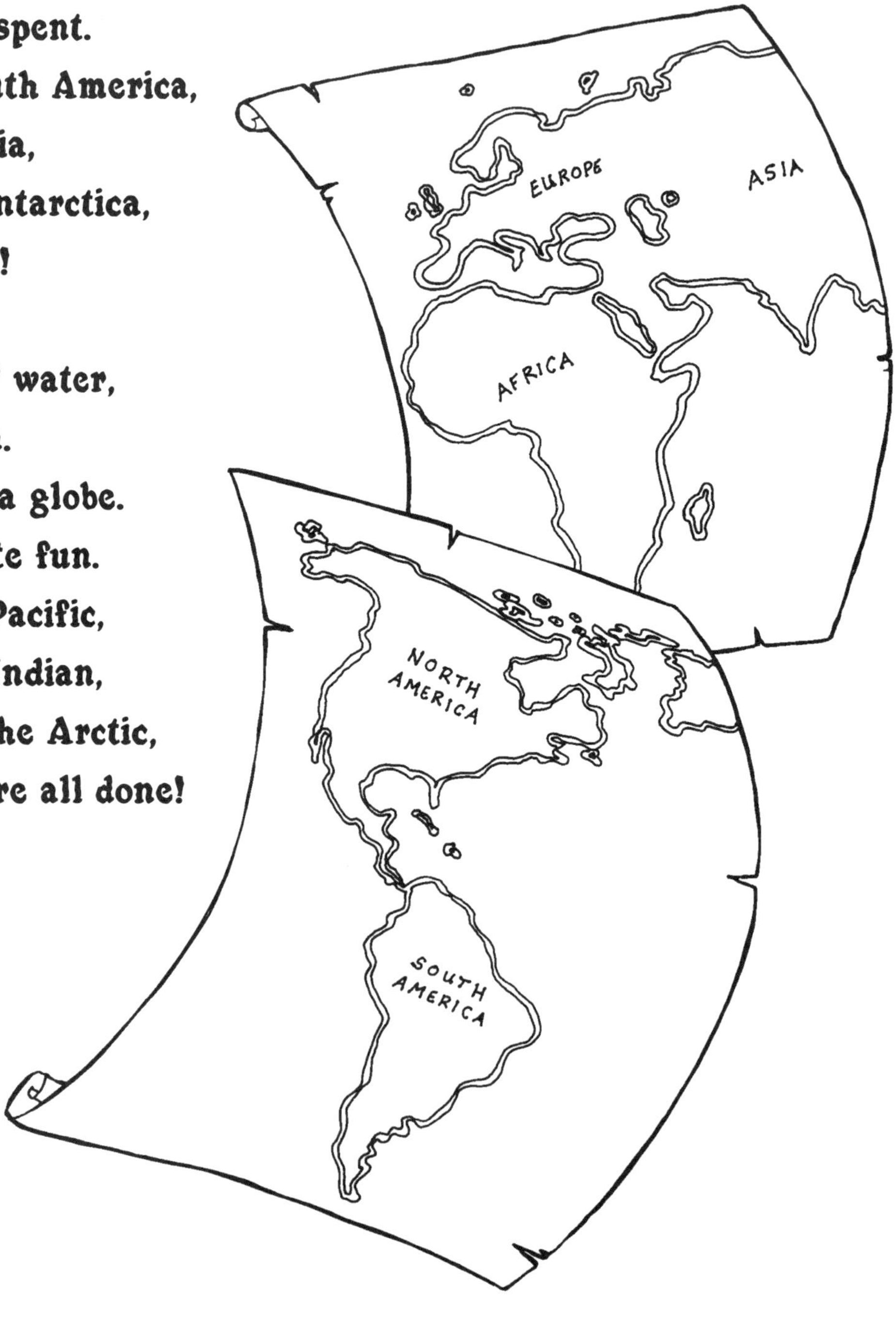

Electrical Safety

Tune "Three Blind Mice"

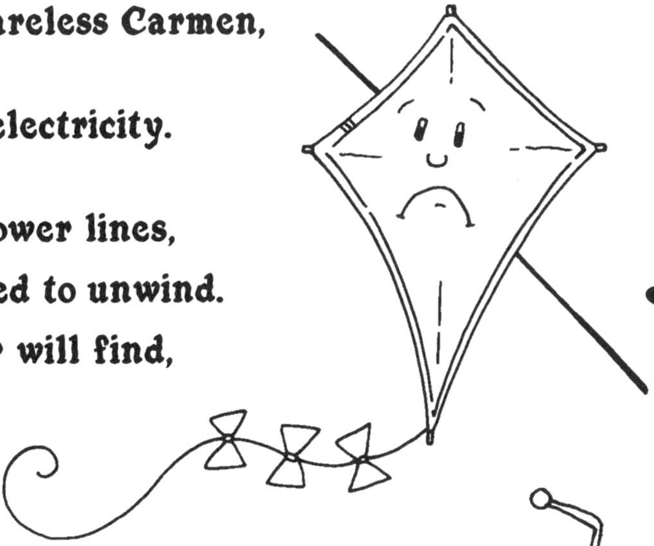

Poor, careless Carmen, poor, careless Carmen,
(Shake head back and forth.)
She was not safe, when using electricity.
(Shake pointer finger.)
She flew her kite 'round the power lines,
It caused a shock when she tried to unwind.
She's the luckiest girl you ever will find,
(Give a relieved look.)
Is poor, careless Carmen.

Silly, dangerous Doug, silly, dangerous Doug,
(Shake head back and forth.)
He was not safe, when using electricity.
(Shake pointer finger.)
His radio was plugged in when he bathed,
It was close but luckily he was saved.
When his mom ran in and told him it's not safe,
Oh, silly, dangerous Doug.

Be a smart, clever kid, be a smart, clever kid,
(Nod finger and point to sky.)
Electricity can be so helpful,
And you will be quite thankful.
When you know and understand safety,
Make a plan and you'll be at peace,
We'll work together and can't you see,
We're all smart, clever kids.
(Pump fists high in air.)

Erosion

Tune "Row, Row, Row Your Boat"

Move, move, move the rocks, (Sway back and forth to beat.)
From one place to the other,
That is called erosion,
It all depends on weather!

"For instance!" (Speak the words without a tune.)

Waves can carry small rocks and sand, (Sway back and forth to beat.)
To a place that's all brand new.
Wind, rivers, and glaciers,
All can do it, too!

Fossils

"Old MacDonald Had a Farm" Tune

Have you ever stepped in the mud?
(Stomp foot down.)
Well, I think that you should know!
Your footprint had a great effect,
(Look at bottom of foot.)
Just like long ago!
It's like a fossil, and it's a trace,
(Snap fingers, swaying back and forth.)
Of plants and animals from another time and place.
Oh, fossils are remains of things,
From a long time ago!

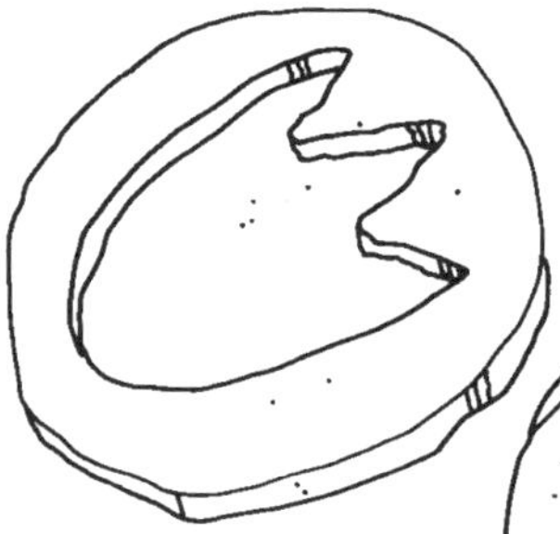

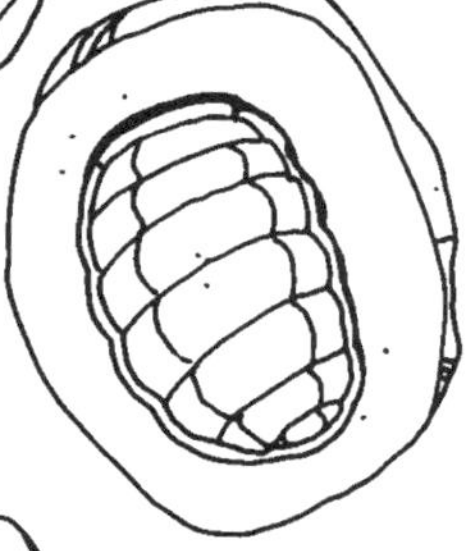

There are clues about Earth's past.
You can observe them for yourself.
By studying fossils and making a guess,
(Point finger to head.)
You need not have to ask
About dinosaurs and fish and trees
(Snap fingers, swaying back and forth.)
Birds and mammals, and even small bees.
Fossils are cool clues that give us a hint
Of how life on Earth was spent! YE-HAW!
(Throw arms high in the air.)

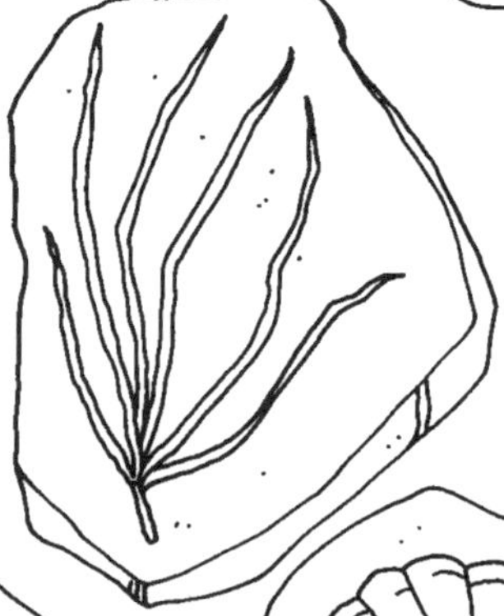

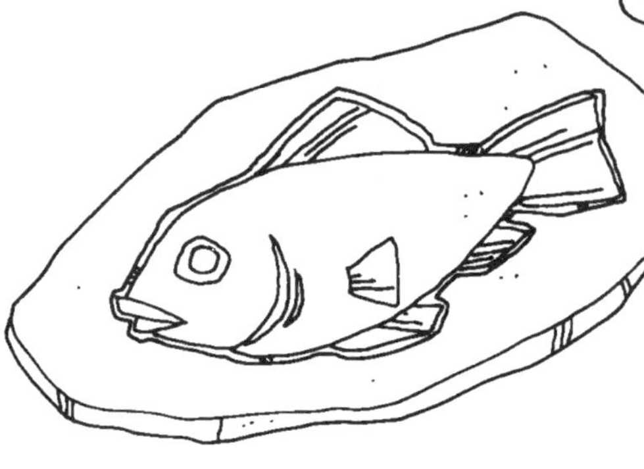

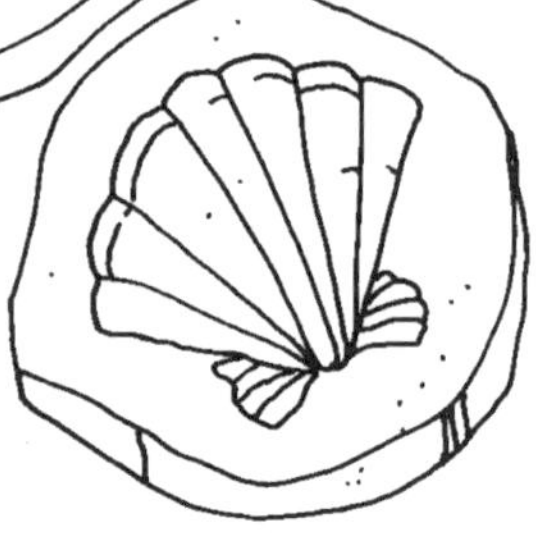

Habitats and Food Chains

Tune "Frère Jacques"

What is habitat, what is habitat?
It's where animals live, animals live!
Water, food, and shelter–
Space is also needed,
For animals to live, in their habitat!

What is a food chain, what is a food chain?
It begins with soil,
Used by plants to grow.
Animals eat the plants.
Droppings, leaves, and fruit all rot.
That makes more soil.
And the chain begins again!

Light

"I've Been Working on the Railroad" Tune

Oh, light is very important!
Light! Helps us see! (Point to eye.)
Oh, light is very important!
Light travels in a beam.
It travels in a straight line, (Extend arm in front of self.)
Until it hits something. (Clap once.)
Oh, yes, light's very important!
Light travels in a beam!

Light can be reflected,
Reflected! Means "bounce off!" (Jump side to side.)
Oh, light can be reflected,
It's what helps us see ourselves. (Pretend to hold mirror in front of self.)
When we're in front of a mirror,
Our reflection is what we see.
Oh, light can be reflected,
I can see my face happy! (Point to your happy smile.)

You might think light has no color,
But that is not so true. (Shake head.)
Oh, light has many, many colors,
There's red, orange, yellow, green, and blue,
Don't forget indigo and violet–
They all mix to form a white light.
Oh, light has many, many colors,
To form a rainbow bright! (Motion arm like a rainbow.)

Magnets

Tune "Oh, My Darling Clementine"

Oh, a magnet, oh, a magnet,
You have two poles; they're north and south.
If they're different, they'll pull together,
If the same, they'll push apart.

Oh, a magnet, oh, a magnet,
You attract so many things,
Like a spoon, nail, or a whistle.
Finding out, what fun it brings!

Magnetism is the force
That is quite invisible!
But we know that it is there,
And it's quite incredible!

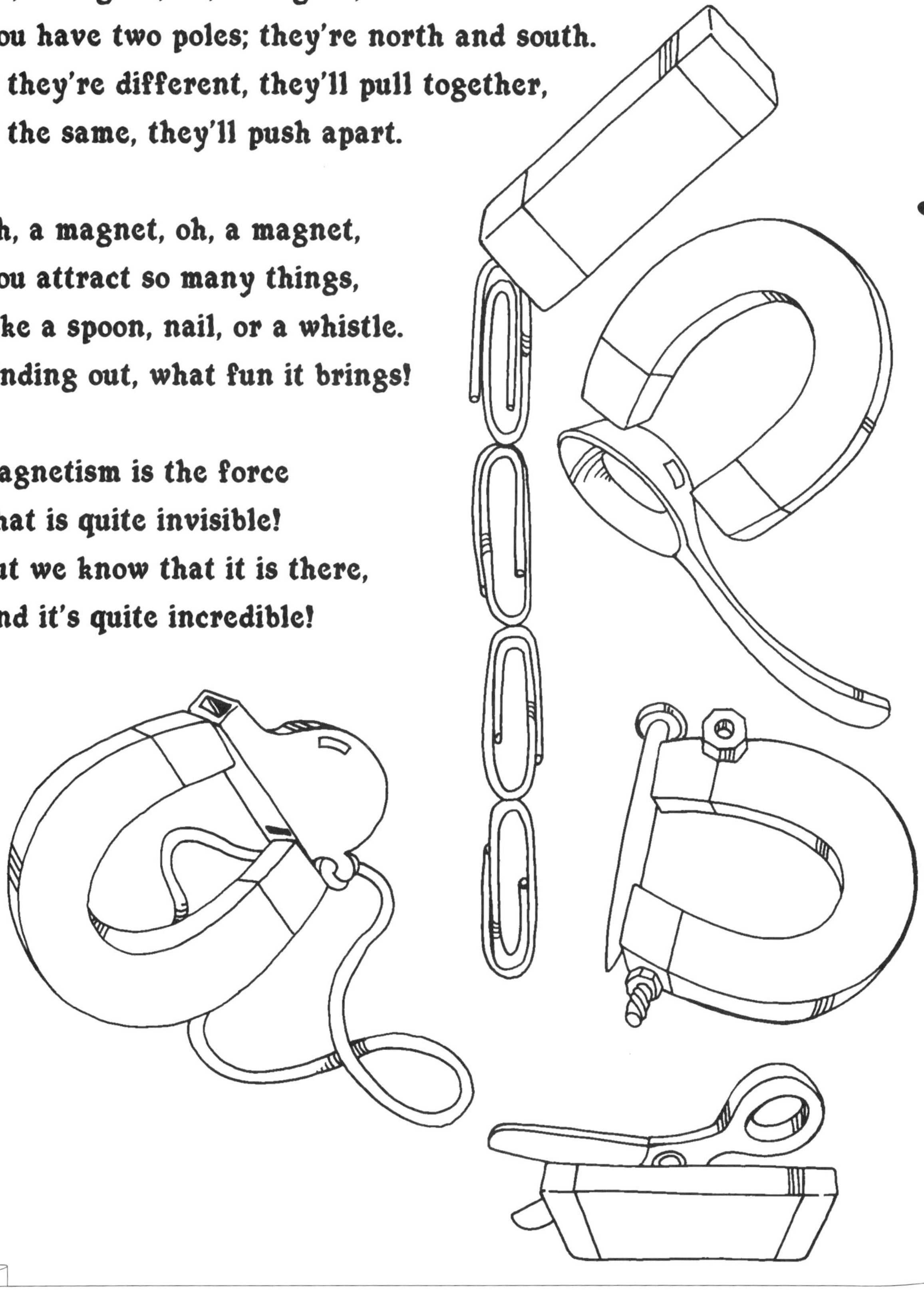

Science

Mammals

Tune: "Army Cadence Chant"

I don't know, but I've been told

Echo: **I don't know, but I've been told**

Mammals are animals, young and old!

Echo: **Mammals are animals, young and old!**

They're warm-blooded, and they've got fur or hair.

Echo: **They're warm-blooded, and they've got fur or hair.**

Their mothers give them milk with care!

Echo: **Their mothers give them milk with care!**

Dogs, cats

Echo: **Monkeys, bats!**

Dolphins, zebras,

Echo: **Whales and cheetahs!**

Don't forget all of us . . . are mammals, too!

Magnificent Mammals

By ____________________

dogs

cats

monkeys

bats

dolphins

zebras

whales

cheetahs

Matter

Tune: "I'm a Yankee Doodle Dandy"

Matter is anything that takes up space,
It has to have some mass to pass.
There are three states of matter that you ought to know,
Solids, and liquids, and gas!
Solids do not change their shape when moved,
Rocks, books, bricks, and balls to name a few,
Liquids do not have a shape to call their very own,
And gas – you may not see, but it's there, too!

We can change our matter to a different form,
By some simple steps you choose to do.
A liquid frozen can turn to ice,
And now you have a solid – it's true!
You can also take that ice and heat it.
Can you think what happens when you do?
The ice will melt and change,
And it's back to where you started,
You boil the liquid and it disappears!

Seasons

Tune: "Take Me Out to the Ball Game"

Take me out during WINTER!
I'll put on my coat, scarf, and hat!
(Act out putting on these clothes.)
I want to build a snowman that's 10 feet tall,
I don't care if I ever see fall. . . .
But then SPRING will come and I'll love it, too,
Flowers will grow and will bloom,

The warmer days are just ahead,
(Bend down and "grow" like a flower.)
And I'll fly my kite instead!
(Act out flying a kite.)

Take me out to the swimming pool!
(Pretend to be swimming.)
SUMMER play is so cool!
(Fan face with hands.)
It's hot and I sweat, but there's always time,
For swimming and diving, I simply don't mind.

But soon comes FALL and I'll love it, too,
I'll start school with a teacher brand-new!
(Point to the teacher.)
For I love, all, the seasons each year,
They make me shout out a cheer!
(Throw arms high in the air.)

HOORAY!

Sensational Seasons

By ____________________

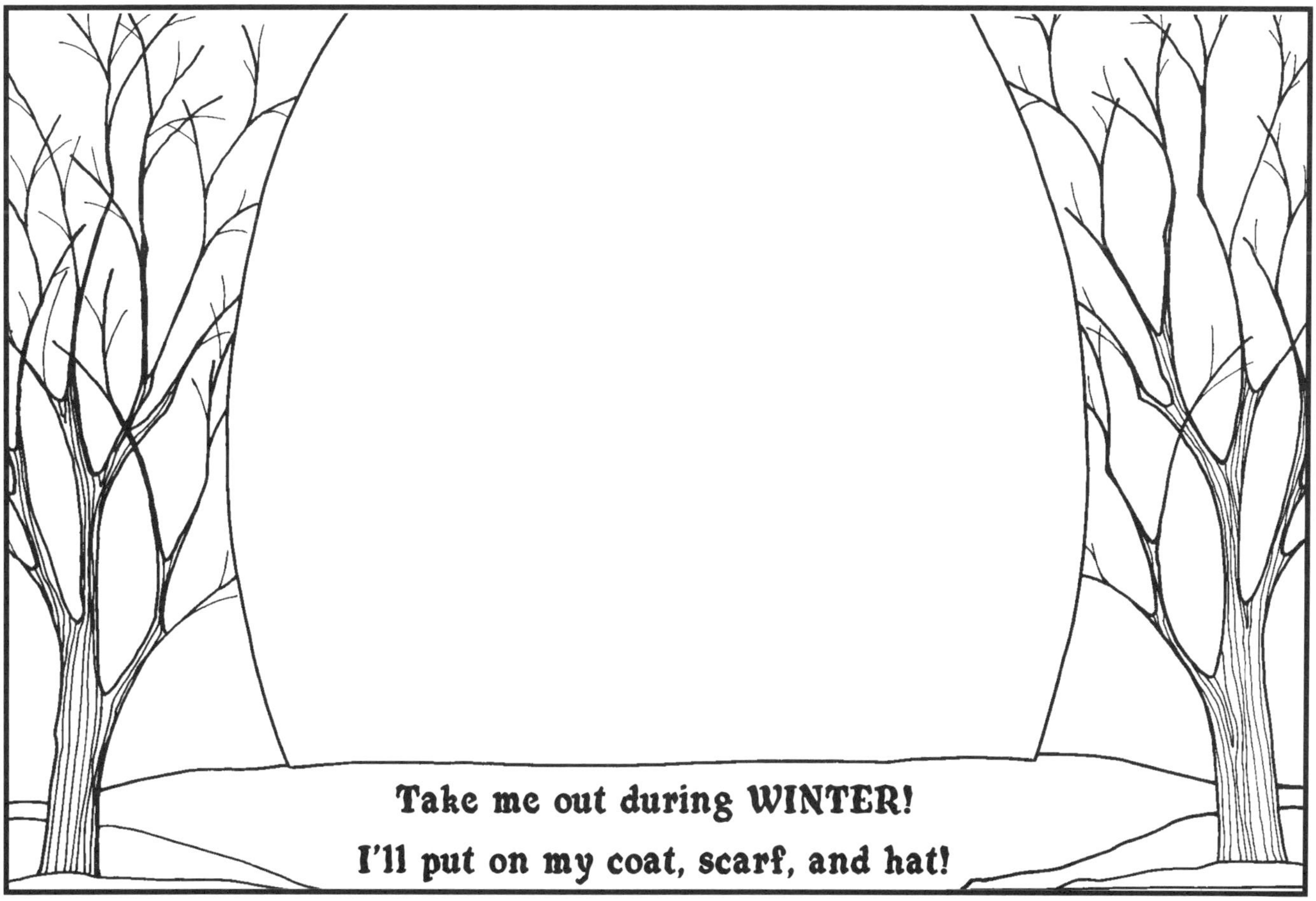

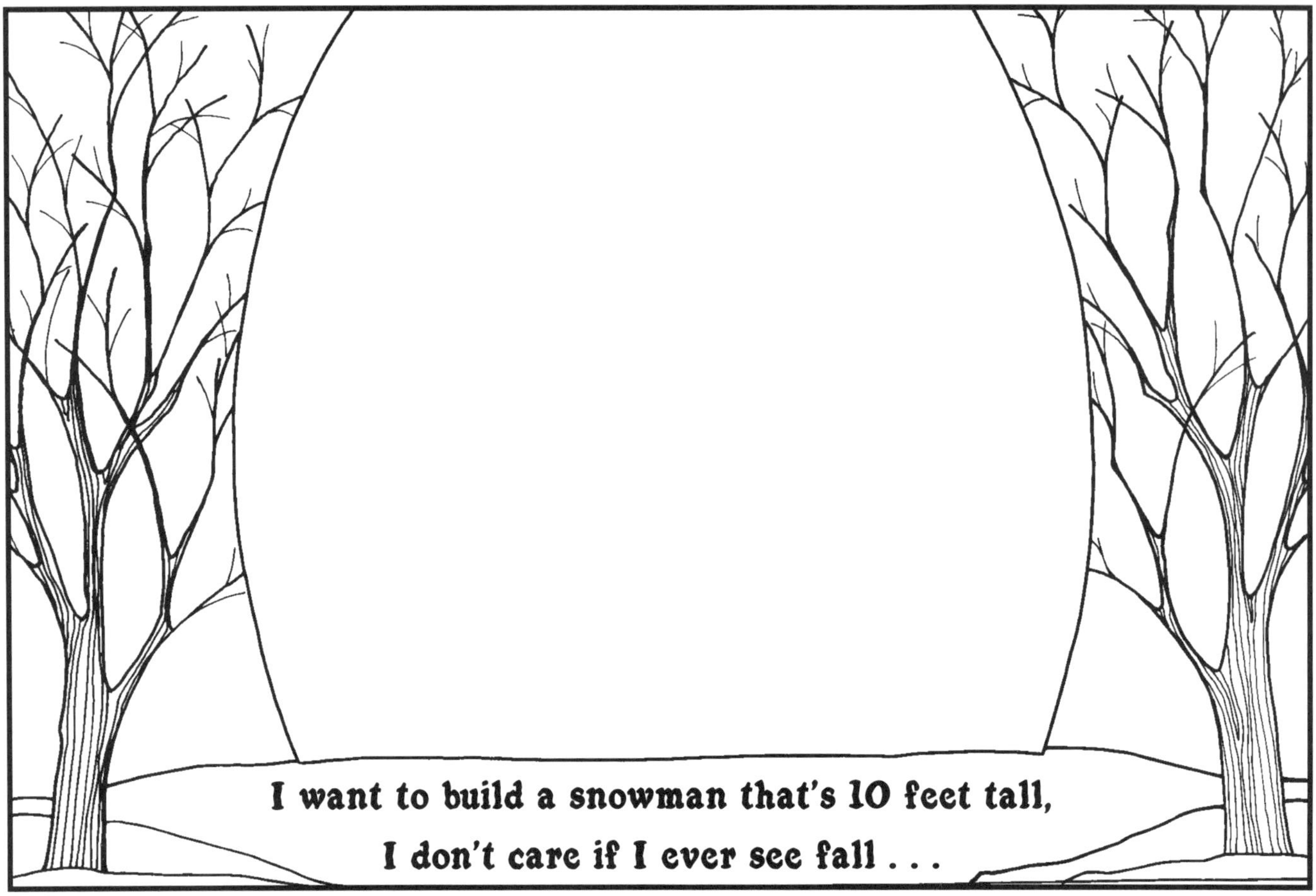
I want to build a snowman that's 10 feet tall,
I don't care if I ever see fall . . .

But then SPRING will come and I'll love it, too,
Flowers will grow and will bloom,

The warmer days are just ahead,
And I'll fly my kite instead!

Take me out to the swimming pool!
SUMMER play is so cool!

It's hot and I sweat, but there's always time,
For swimming and diving, I simply don't mind,

But soon comes FALL and I'll love it, too,
I'll start school with a teacher brand-new!

For I love all the seasons each year,

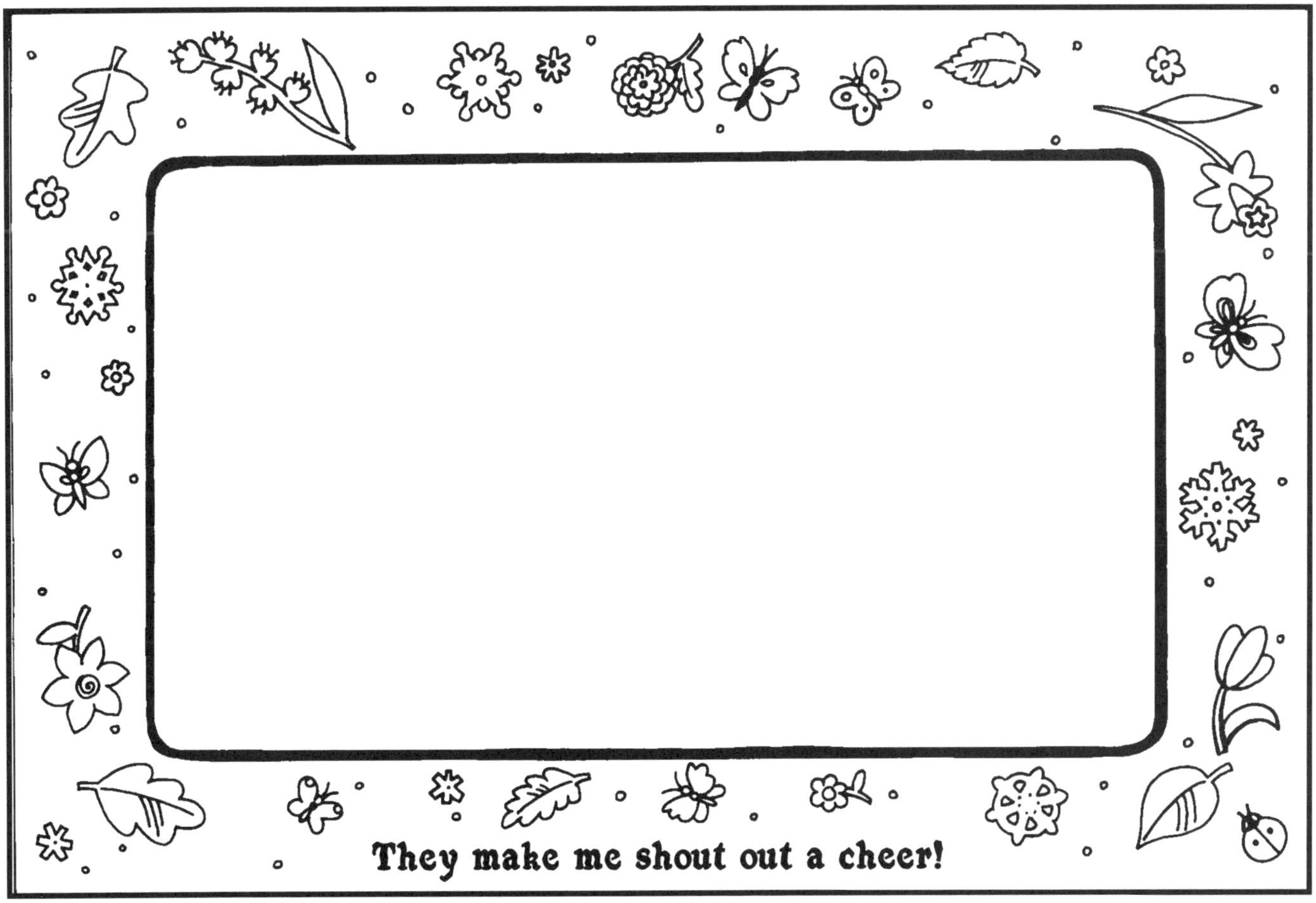

They make me shout out a cheer!

Shadows

"My Bonnie Lies over the Ocean" Tune

My shadow lies upon the sidewalk,
My shadow is something I see,
It happens all during the daytime,
Then at NIGHT my shadow's history!

Bring back, bring back,
Oh, bring back my shadow to me, to me!
Bring back, bring back,
Oh, bring back my shadow to me!

Simple Machines

Tune "Jingle Bells"

Simple machines have one or two parts,
They make life much less hard–
A wheel and axle, a pulley, and screw,
An inclined plane, wedge, and lever, too!

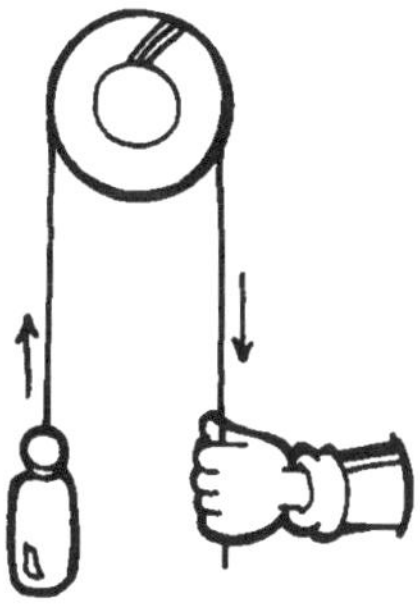

Work is done when force moves things,
It might take a lot of energy.
That's what's great about simple machines,
It makes work seem more of a breeze!

Chorus: (Repeat same chorus tune for rest of song.)
A pulley! A pulley! A wheel and rope to pull things,
The wheel has a groove around its rim,
The rope passes over and pulling begins!

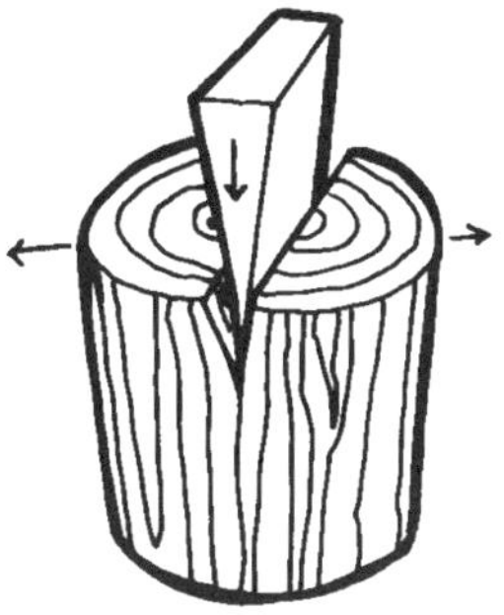

A simple screw! A simple screw!
Holding things together is what it should do,
Lids on jars now hold on tight,
With a simple screw and all its might!

A wedge! A wedge! Sides of a wedge meet at a sharp edge!
People use wedges to split or pierce things,
A nail and a knife are some of those things!

An inclined plane! An inclined plane!
One ends higher—they're not the same,
It's like a ramp to lower or raise,
When hefty moving, we'll sing its praise!

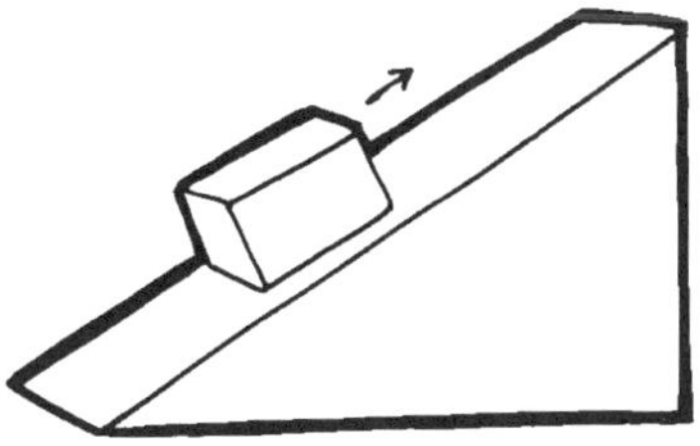

A lever! A lever! Has three parts—the force, fulcrum, and load!
Some include a shovel and pliers,
A wheelbarrow and a seesaw board!

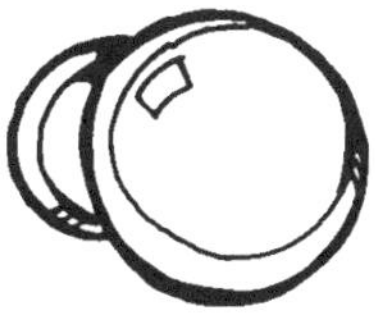

A wheel and axle! A wheel and axle!
They're connected and around it goes!
A doorknob is the perfect thing,
A wheel and axle is what it means!

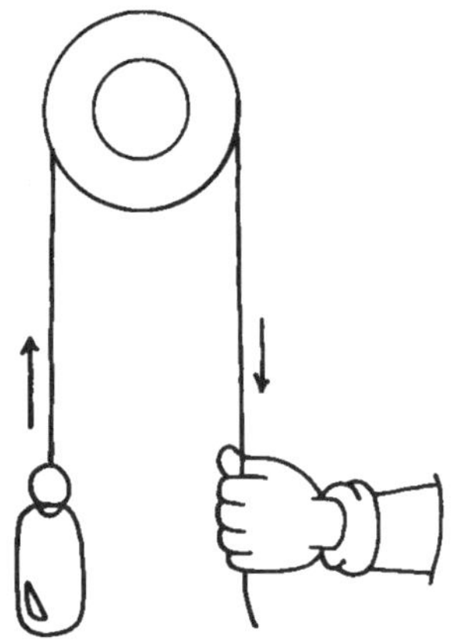

A pulley

A screw

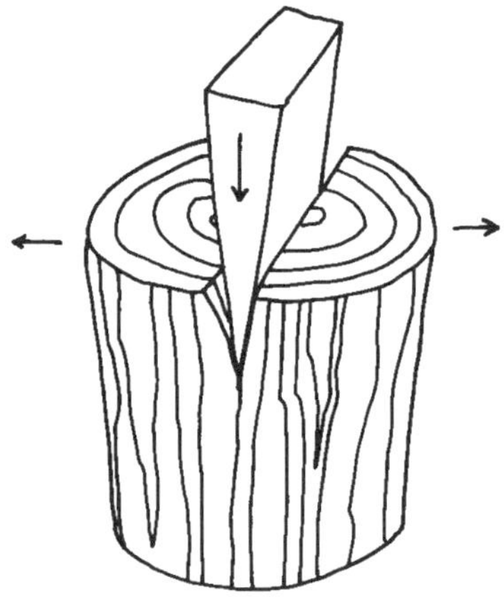

A wedge

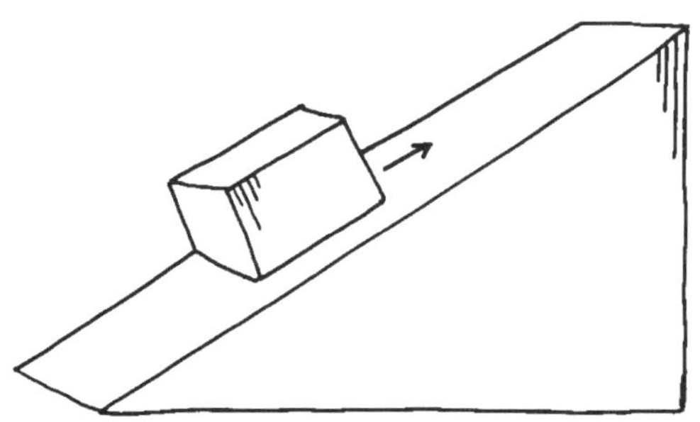

An inclined plane

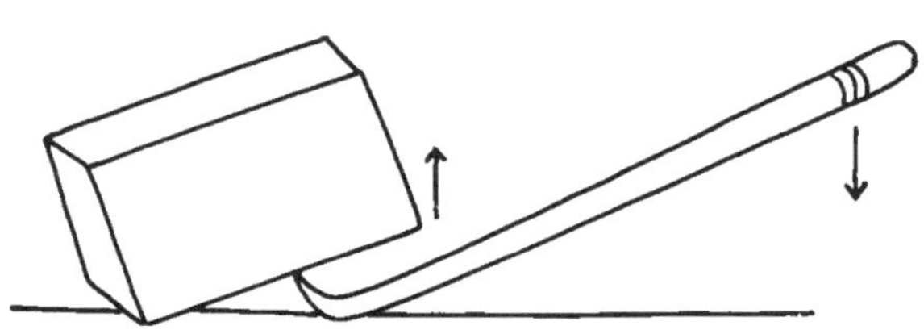

A lever

A wheel and axle

Taking a Raindrop Through the Water Cycle

Tune "I've Been Working on the Railroad"

I am just a little raindrop
Falling from a cloud, so high up.
I am just a little raindrop
Just waitin' my turn to plop, plop, PLOP, PLOP!
(Jump up and down four times.)
First, I evaporate from the ocean,
(Bring raindrop to the sky.)
Then cool off during condensation,
("Squeeze" the clouds in the sky.)
Then I fall as rain or snow,
(Bring the raindrop down like rain.)
And begin the cycle again. AS YOU KNOW!
(Swing arm around and point to front.)

Water

Tune: "Frère Jacques"

We need water, we need water,
For all things, for all things,
Like drinking, washing, and cooking,
For animals and many jobs,
Gardens and crops, gardens and crops.

The Water Cycle

Tune: "Frère Jacques"

Evaporation! Condensation!	(Move arms up toward the sky.)
And clouds form,	(Squeeze "clouds" in the sky.)
In the sky,	
Next precipitation,	(Trickle fingers down like rain.)
Then accumulation,	(Make "waves" with arms.)
'Round and 'round,	
The water cycle.	(Move arms around in a circle.)

More About the Water Cycle!

Tune: "London Bridge Is Falling Down"

Evaporation, rising up,
To the sky,
From the earth.
Condensation forms the clouds,
That cause precipitation.

Precipitation's when it rains,
Or it snows,
Or falls as sleet.
Accumulation collects it all,
And the cycle begins again!

Tools to Measure and Predict Weather

Science

Tune: "Home on the Range"

Oh, give me a tool that will help me in school,
To record the weather outside.
I just want to know—will it rain, shine, or snow?
Is there something that's tested and tried?

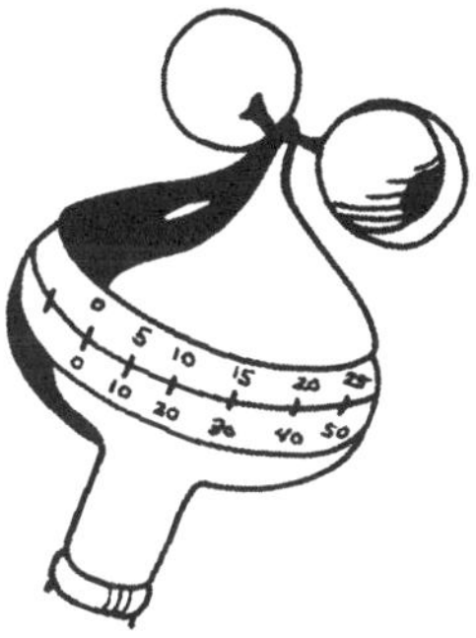

Anemometers measure the wind speed,
A wind vane shows where it goes.
Barometers measure the outside air pressure,
A rain gauge holds rain, sleet, or snow!

Oh, these tools are so great but hold on, now wait!
There is more to weather than that!
Other things there must be, we can use as our key,
And help us with our outside forecast!

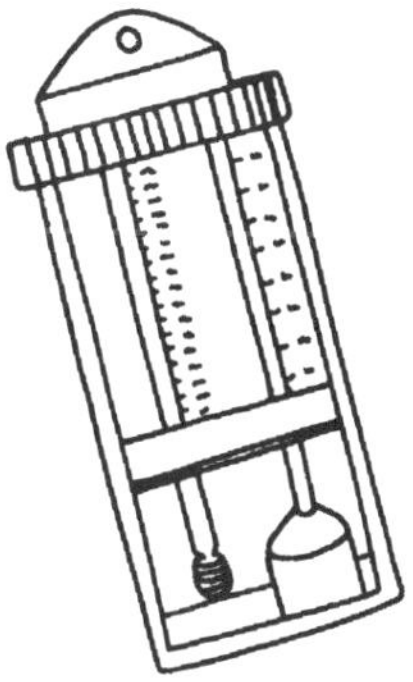

Thermometers measure the temperature,
Hygrometers test humidity,
Weather balloons,
Satellite and radar,
Now understanding weather is easy for me!

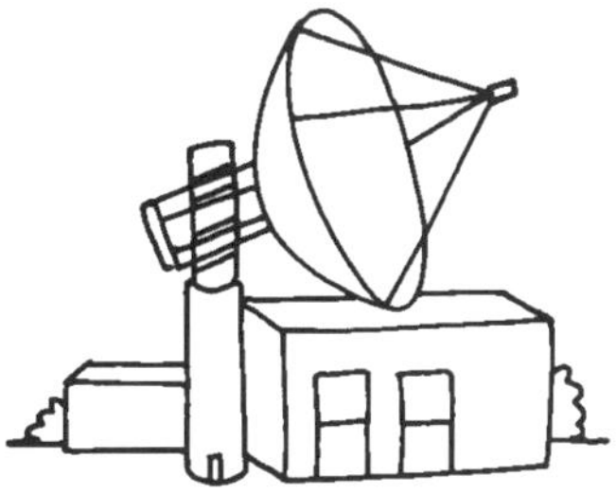

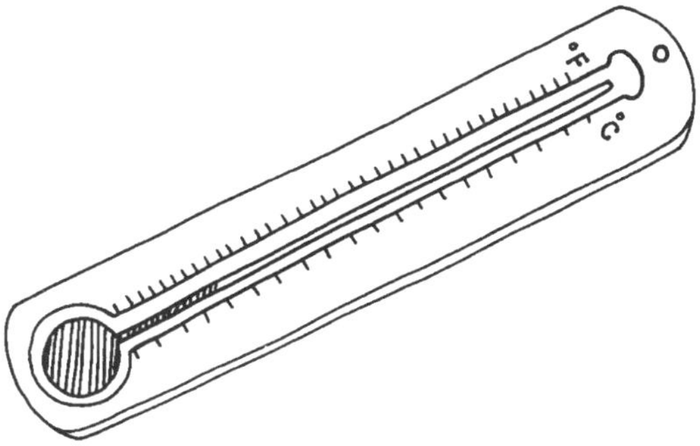

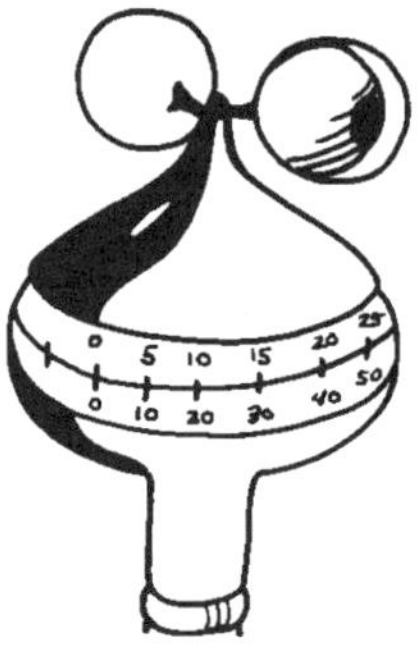

An anemometer

A wind vane

A barometer

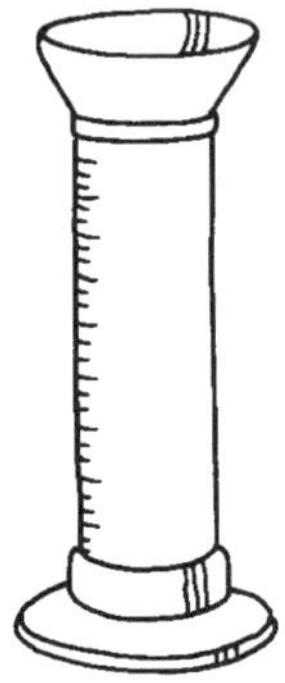

A rain gauge

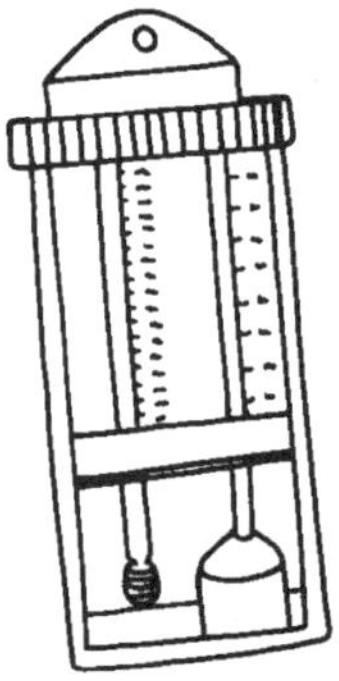

A hygrometer

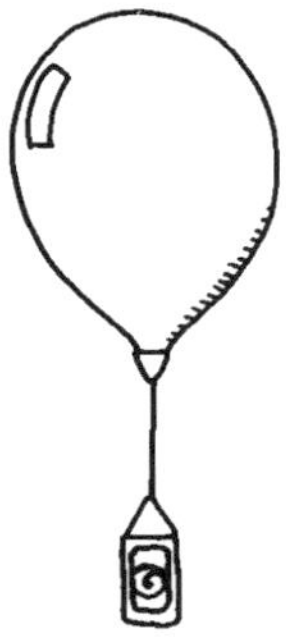

A weather balloon

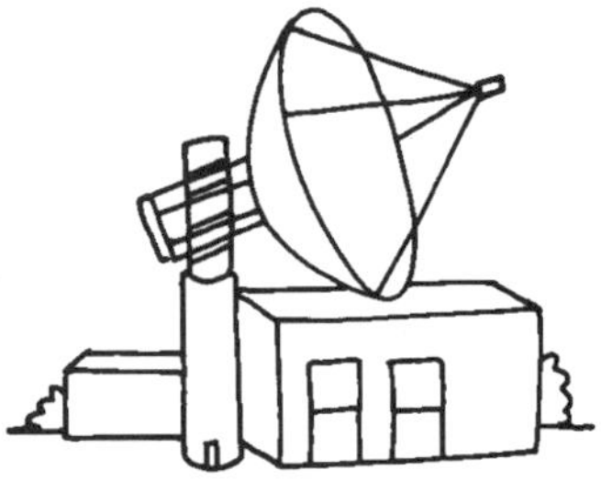

Radar

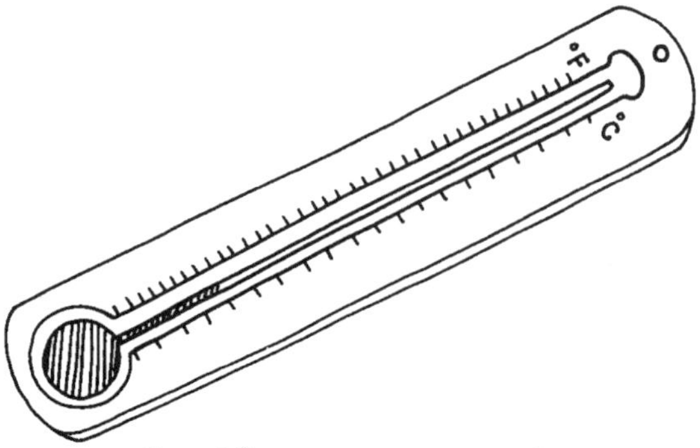

A thermometer